Helping You is Killing Me
The Armorbearers Call to Serve

By Everett Gates

Helping You is Killing Me
The Armorbearers Call to Serve
by Everett Gates

Printed in the United States of America

ISBN 978-1-60647-295-8

E-mail: EKAKEGATES@aol.com

www.xulonpress.com

ENDORSEMENTS

I want to personally commend my brother Everett for having the courage and foresight in approaching this all important area of Ministry in the early days of this twenty-first century.

"Helping You Is Killing Me" is a must read book that every serious Armorbearer should read, analyze and take careful note of the principles and concerns that Everett took the time and the pain to mention in this writing.

All of us in ministry, and Armorbearers in particular, would do well to learn from Everett's errors and pay attention to his advice.

> Bishop Neil C. Ellis
> Senior Pastor
> Mount Tabor Full Gospel
>   Baptist Church
> Nassau Bahamas

One of the greatest tools of servanthood and leadership is sacrifice. If you're not willing to say to God "Kill me so I can live," then you're not ready for this book. Pastor Everett takes us on a journey that photographs how to serve, lead, submit, love and give in the Kingdom of God. If you are struggling with any of these photographs, listen to what Everett has to say. Not only will it bless you, it will encourage and motivate you. A must read!

> Dr. Wanda A. Davis Turner
> Preacher, Author, Musician

Everett Gates has written a practical but very real manual on the role of armor bearer. As stated, the idea of serving has fallen out of favor. Yet God is calling many to serve. Through this book those burdened to serve can find hope and fulfillment in their call. The words written here are from a man who walks this passion daily. This book is a life manual from a man who has lived the life.

> Dr. J. Martin Taylor
> Administrative Bishop
> Church of God in Florida

Everett Gates taps into the great mystery of servanthood—revealing the joy and depths of a life of blessings and contentment. Searching hearts of armorbearers, Everett's life lessons prepare and equip those choosing this high call, as well as bring encouragement and restoration to the most fainthearted. As a pastor, I have been the recipient of the prayers and support of so many who have stood in the gap for me, my family, and the Body of Christ and know and appreciate firsthand the sacrifices made by these great men and women. Tools like this one are essential for the building up of the saints for the work of ministry. I am thankful for this man of God, who not only chose to make this journey, but who has consistently stood through adversity in order for the Kingdom of God to advance on the earth.

Bishop Jim Bolin
Senior Pastor, Trinity Chapel
Powder Springs, GA

If you have a desire to be great in the Kingdom of God, you must first become a servant which is what you will find in "Helping You Is Killing Me." With a clear and precise understanding, Everett Gates enlightens us on the power and pitfalls of being a servant. Penned with hands that have years of experience, this book is no theory, but a reality. I highly recommend this book to those striving to become great in the Kingdom of God.

Bishop Chris Dutruch
Senior Pastor, Celebration of
Praise
Clermont, Florida

Acknowledgements

To my wife, Kateena, thank you for being such a wonderful example of a true servant. Thank you for standing in the gap, praying and loving me through all the stages and challenges that we have endured in life. I love you. To my children, Alexis, Kendra, and Everett, thank you for being such wonderful children. You are indeed a blessing. I love you so much. To my mother, Thelma Gates, who prayed the prayer of Hannah and said "Lord, if you give me a son, I will give him back to you," thank you for being a praying woman of God. I love you. Finally, thanks to my father, Earl Gates, and my siblings, Ivorie Gates and Cynthia Morgan, for praying for me continuously. Even when I wanted to throw in the towel, you told me to trust God and to stay focused. I love you.

Table of Contents

Dedication

To the one who is contemplating quitting and
leaving your god-given assignment, looking for
affirmation, encouragement and acceptance,
your life does matter. God has a plan for you.

And to all who has been hurt,
while functioning in your purpose

May you find the strength and courage to go on
and trust Him who has called you
for such a time as this.

Preface

No matter what position of service you hold in your church, on your job or in your community, you may be wondering, "Why should I read this book? How can it help me?" Let's just say chances are I have been where you are and can relate to your issues and challenges. As I once did, have you ever thought about quitting and throwing in the towel because helping others has taken a toll on you? Have you ever felt like your life didn't matter, but you knew that God gave you a promise? Have you ever been hurt while trying to do what God called you to do, yet knew deep within that He gave you that assignment? Have you felt like others have taken you for granted? Do you feel unappreciated? If so, this book is for you.

Helping You is Killing Me will encourage you to hold on to your promise and cling to your dream, vision, and purpose. Don't quit. Don't leave. Don't stop pushing. Don't stop serving. Most importantly, don't step outside of God's will for your life. This is a test!

The Church in America has allowed the enemy to creep into our midst and turn us into selfish, greedy people, which has immobilized us and rendered us ineffective. As a result, many have lost their joy. Others have seen their passion and zeal dwindle. Given this picture, the question is whether you *really* want your life to matter. On the day of Christ's return, do you want to hear Him say: "Well done, good and faithful servant?" If so, you need to read this book. It will help you find the strength you need to stay focused on your assignment. And, provide the tools and strategies you need to gain victory over the devil's schemes.

What the Church needs and what America needs is people with the courage to tell God, "Kill me so that I can live." As Jesus says in Matthew 10:39, "Whoever finds his life will lose it, and whoever loses his life for my sake will find it." This truth leaves you to ponder such weighty questions as:

1. Do I want to live or die?
2. Do I want success or significance?
3. Do I want to _____? (Fill in the blank.)
4. How desperate am I to walk in my purpose?

Matthew 23:11 says, "The greatest among you will be your servant." Yet, as Christians march through the twenty-first century, our pastors are dying, churches are splitting, leaders are being exposed and ridiculed, and marriages are being destroyed—all because no one wants to die to self in order to serve. This book is about serving, giving, and submitting. We need people who will declare, "Enough is enough." Are you that kind of gutsy individual who is prepared to make a difference and stop the devil from causing Christ's followers so much trouble? If so, you have purchased the right book. Let's get started.

—Everett Gates

Chapter 1

Down but not Out

Adecade had passed since I felt God calling me to serve the pastor of my church by becoming his armorbearer. Just as Aaron and Hur held up Moses' arms in the battle with the Amalekites (Exodus 17), I was willing to tackle any task, no matter how menial; fetch anything he needed, no matter how small; and serve as his confidante, which includes a willingness to hear the most personal of details without revealing these secrets to another living soul. When I started in my early 20's, the church saw anywhere from 300 to 500 people on a Sunday. Over ten years it had swollen to over 15,000, growth that had multiplied the demands on my time and me personally.

The stress grew so intense that, at its peak, my cardiologist referred me for some tests at a hospital. When my pastor showed up to see me, I lay back on my bed, trying to stifle the pain and brewing emotions that I feared would explode all over the room. Finally, taking a deep breath, I said, "You know, helping you is killing me."

He responded with that typical, hearty, booming chuckle that had endeared so many faithful followers to his charismatic leadership. That is, until he saw that I wasn't smiling. His face suddenly subdued, he asked, "What do you mean by that statement?"

"Pastor, I'm smiling on the outside," I said, sighing. "But I'm dying on the inside."

Whose fault was it? Nobody's. And everybody's. Including mine. Because I had never been exposed to a situation where an average-sized, relatively unknown congregation mushroomed to a megachurch of national influence, I didn't realize how much my assignment had changed. As growth swelled attendance and the size of our buildings, I failed to recognize the corresponding increase in the demands of my position. Not just the hours I had to spend at the office, but the time I had to spend on the road. As my pastor's profile increased, we would be gone for up to five days a week, weeks at a time, traveling to all areas of the nation and sometimes beyond. Wherever he spoke, I was there. This went on for years.

As the church grew, so did the pressures of being in a visible position. The closer I grew to my leader, the more I knew. As a consequence, more people wanted to hang out with me. Because of the confidential nature of much of what I learned, I had to exercise care in forming relationships. When I discovered that a number of people pretended to like me because they wanted "inside information" on the pastor or the ministry, I retreated further into my shell. It didn't help that envious and jealous people spread empty gossip about me. The pressure cooker of my job slowly led to migraine headaches, dizzy spells, stomach pangs, nightmares, and nervousness. Eventually, it negatively affected my eating habits, sleep patterns, and marriage.

Although I still felt assured of my divine call to serve God as an armorbearer, I wasn't spiritually prepared for the task. While I enjoyed serving and seeing my pastor succeed, I failed to appreciate that I wasn't taking care of myself. I had allowed myself to lose sight of what I was called to do—hold up my pastor's arms. That was impossible to do when my own arms were slowly falling to the side.

I know my story is not unique. I still meet armor-bearers who are burning the candle at both ends, which leaves them feeling drained and ineffective. Yet while they are dying a slow death of frustration and emotional overload, they proclaim they are "helping" their leader. I always ask them such questions as, "What good does it do your leader for you to sink into weakness and burnout? What can an insecure armorbearer do for his leader? What can a hospitalized armorbearer do for his leader?" And, in the most extreme cases, "What can a dead armor-bearer do for his leader?"

Before I scare you away from this position of fulfillment and service, let me caution: Learn from my mistakes. Find the strength you need to hold up your pastor's arms. Most importantly, in the midst of serving, take care of yourself and your family. Don't allow ministry to become misery.

Ignorance Affects the Church

"My people are destroyed for lack of knowledge..." (Hosea 4:6).

My ignorance of the need for spiritual growth and balance in my life could have destroyed my life and ruined my destiny as an armorbearer. However, there is another form of ignorance afflicting the American church that has lulled us into an unhealthy state where we have lost sight of the necessity—and the exalted state—of servanthood. This is dangerous. Ignorance can immobilize us, causing us to remain passive because we fail to understand what it accomplishes. It gives the devil an opening, allowing him the freedom to pursue and conquer without being noticed. When we fail to discern the enemy's plans, it negatively affects our purposes, lives, homes, relationships, marriages, and churches.

In this book I want to make you aware of how, through ignorance of servanthood, we have allowed the devil to creep into our midst and turn us into selfish, greedy people. No one wants to serve. Instead, everyone wants to be served, which is the by-product of an independent spirit. Serving has become a "bad" thing, even though Matthew 23:11 says, "The greatest among you will be your servant." Since Christ made that statement, how have we come to look on service as a bad quality? When did greatness fall into disfavor?

Our pastors are suffering because no one wants to serve. Men and women of God, who have been called to bring forth a Word from God, face slander, exposure, ridicule, temptation, and lures to immorality. Often, because we have left them uncovered. The independent spirit has tricked us, preventing us from serving, praying for, and covering the one whom God has called us to serve, the person to whom we owe submission. This leads us to contradict the sound advice of Hebrews 13:17: "Obey them that have the rule over you, and submit yourselves: for they watch for your souls, as they that must give account, that they may do it with joy, and not with grief: for that is unprofitable for you."

Submit. That is a word you don't hear much today. No one wants to submit; everyone wants to be in charge. In the meantime, the church is going to hell in a hand-basket because everyone is thinking about himself or herself. Our leaders are dying prematurely. They have been left out in the cold for the enemy. I heard Paul Cole—son of famed men's ministry leader Edwin Louis Cole—once say, "Either you will be tested on that which you teach, or you will teach on that which you have been tested."

The reason I am ready to write this book is that I have passed some tests and failed others, which helped equip me to share my story. I can tell others what it means to be an armorbearer, without speaking from hurt and pain. I almost allowed my past pain to hinder me from operating in my calling. I know that I am called to serve and I am comfortable with answering that call.

I am writing this book to encourage my fellow armorbearers and tell them to hang in there when everything seems to be chaotic. Cover your pastor even if you are tired and growing weary. Why? Because pastors need you. They need your prayers and support, your eyes and your ears. Don't let them fall. Besides, if the truth be told, you need your pastor. You need him or her to boldly stand and declare the word of the Lord. You need pastors to take their rightful place and kick the devil's butt. Likewise, your pastor needs you to take your rightful place, and that is to stand alongside him or her, winning souls for God's Kingdom.

I am one of you. I am a servant, an armorbearer. I love it. I also understand how you may want to throw in the towel and call it quits, but you can't. I understand the loneliness and most (if not all) of the struggles you face, such as lack of appreciation and discouragement. But you can't quit. Why? Because it is your life and your purpose for being on this earth. Believe me, I have wanted to quit many times and God wouldn't allow me. He is looking for men and women like me and you to cover His mouthpiece.

Significant Assignment

Most armorbearers think that their assignment is insignificant. But that's not true. I used to often hear my former pastor, ask, "When you die, will it matter that you were even born?" Wow! That was a life-changing question because I wanted my life to matter. I wanted to make an impact in this world. Most people look at those who are out front. Often, the most important people are those in the background, making everything work and bringing it all together. This is what armorbearers do. We make our leader look good. If you can't handle a lack of praise because you desire the limelight, you're in the wrong place. I find great wisdom in a statement I once read: "It takes a greater man to make another man great."

After serving in ministry for several years, I went to talk to another pastor. I told him that I was tired of church and serving because it was killing me. As I mentioned earlier, as an armorbearer I had experienced chest pains, migraine headaches, dizzy spells, and skin rashes, symptoms that constantly sent me to the hospital. These stress-related ailments had drained me. (Of course, the problem was I was serving in my own strength, not relying on God to carry me through. I had to learn to trust and depend on Him even to be a servant.)

I went to this pastor because I knew I could confide in him. I knew that he would listen and tell me the truth, not just what I wanted to hear. When it came time for him to respond, I almost expected him to say something like, "I was wondering what took you so long to leave." Instead, he gazed at me and said, "Wipe your tears and dry your face. I have some bad news for you. Son, you will serve in the church again and you will serve pastors, because that's who you are. That's who God created you to be."

When I heard those words, I almost felt like slitting my wrists. I was devastated and angry at God. I was not only tired of church, but the people in it. Although I knew service was my calling, I no longer wanted to do it and I definitely didn't want to hear that truth. I wanted to escape it and do something else. I wanted out of ministry.

Seeing the emotion surging in my countenance, he cautioned me to calm down and think for a moment.

"Ask yourself: Do you enjoy serving?" he said.

As I listened for God's voice, I had to admit that I did. While I love serving, the challenges I faced originated with weariness. I was tired of the games, manipulation, and drama that seemed to be a natural part of megachurch life. Still, I heard God whisper, "You are on an assignment from Me, not man." He reminded me that He created me to do this. So, after I pulled myself together, I had to admit that despite all the pain, rejection, and disappointment, there was no greater joy than serving.

How strange! How could I have joy when I was experiencing so much pain and anxiety? That sounds like a contradiction, but serving is what fulfilled me, even with all the other things that come with it. Everyone on this earth is called to do something and that is what I am called to do. And, if you're reading this book, you're probably called to do the same thing: Serve! You are an armorbearer.

What's in a Name?

Where did the word, "armorbearer," come from? In 1 Samuel 16:21 we read, "David came to Saul and entered his service. Saul liked him very much, and David became one of his armor-bearers." What does an armorbearer do? In Old Testament times, the armorbearer carried his leader's shield into battle. He had the privilege and responsibility of seeing to his leader's safety. In recent times I have frequently heard about great men and women of God who have fallen into immorality, quit the ministry, or gotten entangled in other sad events. This greatly disturbs me. I wonder:

- ✓ Where are the men and women who have been called to stand in the gap?
- ✓ Where are the "called out" ones, who are supposed to cover and protect their pastor?

✓ Who is praying for pastors and holding them accountable?

✓ Where are those who are called to hold up their pastor's arms?

✓ Where are the armorbearers?

This book is written to encourage those who have been called to hold up their pastor's arms. It's written to those who are growing weary, but know deep within themselves that this is their calling. It's written to the person who wants to throw in the towel, yet knows that he or she is on an assignment from God. Listen. You can't quit. You have got to step up to the plate and cover your pastor. God will see you through.

Regardless of what happens in life and the circumstances you face, you have been called to do what you do. You have been called to serve with loyalty, commitment, and faithfulness. Others may not understand why you do what you do. Why should you go the extra mile in making sure that your pastor is taken care of? Why should you stay up in the late night hours to pray for and cover your pastor? I too had to deal with my flesh when it came to submitting to my pastor, but I had to die to self. Don't make the same mistakes I made. I murmured and complained about my situation instead of expressing my concerns to God. Keep your head up and find like-minded people.

Psalms 1:1-2 says, "Blessed is the man who does not walk in the counsel of the wicked or stand in the way of sinners or sit in the seat of mockers. But his delight is in the law of the Lord, and on his law he meditates day and night." This verse shows how you need the counsel of God's Word and wise people. Never surround yourself with "yes men" who always agree with you. You need people around you who are going to tell you the truth. The church needs you. The body of Christ needs you. Your pastor needs you. You have a calling.

In the late 1980's, I was called to serve a pastor for the first time. I wanted nothing more than to see him succeed. I knew that if he succeeded, I succeeded. I wanted nothing more than to see this man blessed and walking in God's favor. I wanted his dreams to come to pass. As long as I was doing what God had called me to do by serving him, I knew that my dreams would come to pass. A verse that became particularly meaningful to me during that time is found in Luke 16:12: "And if you have not been trustworthy with someone else's property, who will give you property of your own?"

There are other reasons that I was so sold out in making sure that he was taken care of? Yes, I wanted him to succeed and be victorious in every area of his life. There are six reasons:

1. I knew that God called me to serve him and cover him in prayer.
2. I knew that he cared for me and my dreams.
3. I knew that no matter what happened, he was going to be there for me.
4. I knew that he genuinely loved me, and not just for what I could do for him.

5. I knew that he wanted me to succeed in my gifts and talents.
6. I knew that he constantly prayed for me and my family. At times, you would have thought that he was *my* armorbearer.

David as an Armorbearer

When we consider this office, a good role model is David when he served as an armorbearer. In 1 Samuel 16:14-23, King Saul was troubled and distressed in his spirit, so he decided to find a skillful musician. When anxious or disturbed, he needed a person who could help ease his pain and state of mind. One of his servants made a recommendation. In 1 Samuel 16:18 (KJV) it says, "Behold, I have seen a son of Jesse the Bethlehemite, that is…:"

1. Cunning in playing
2. A mighty valiant man
3. A man of war
4. Prudent in matters
5. A comely person
6. And the Lord was with him.

Saul loved him greatly. You will notice that David was a skillful musician, a bold and brave man of courage, a warrior yet careful in speech, handsome, and most importantly, knew God's presence. Now that you have read these biblical descriptions of a true armorbearer, where could you use some help?

In addition, an armorbearer must be concerned with appearance, not for the sake of "looking good," but because it reflects on your pastor. Your pastor is not going to want you walking around dressed haphazardly. You must carry yourself well. You must know how to talk when guests are present, when to speak and when to sit back and listen, and when to exit the room. You must dress nicely, be well groomed, and project a pleasant appearance. You can't have your pants hanging down below your butt and call yourself an armorbearer. You can't be afraid to stand up and be bold and courageous when the time comes for you to stand. And most of all, you must have the Lord with you.

I know many people who call themselves armorbearers, but don't possess any of these qualifications. Yes, they may be handsome and have nice clothes, but that is about all. Anybody can groom himself or herself and acquire fashionable attire, but do you have courage to stand in the midst of challenges? Are you bold enough to face adversity and stay the course? Is the Lord with you? Are you seeking the Lord for His guidance? If not, you're in the way. Get yourself trained or get out of the way. Time is too short to be playing around. Our leaders are dying. I'm not just talking about physically, but spiritually. Why? Because they are growing weary from having to carry too many burdens.

Another example of an armorbearer's loyalty is found in Judges 9:45-55, which describes the death of Abimelech. During war, Abimelech was on the verge of seizing the city. He had the enemy on the run and was ready to burn the tower down where many of the people had taken cover. Yet, before he could achieve victory, as his forces lay wood at the foot of the tower, a lady threw down a millstone and struck Abimelech in the head, cracking his skull. Then, "hurriedly he called to his armor-bearer, 'Draw your sword and kill me, so that they can't say, "A woman killed him." (Judges. 9:54.)

Although Abimelech was wicked and not a man easily served, he had a loyal armorbearer. He was the person closest to Abimelech. Since Abimelech's armorbearer did not want it said that a woman killed his master, he obeyed his leader. Hearing the order that was given, verse 54 concludes, "So his servant ran him through, and he died."

As I read about Saul and his armorbearer, and then Abimelech and his armorbearer, I asked myself if I could be like them. David's story especially touched my heart. He had an opportunity to kill Saul, but didn't. What an example of faithfulness. He was a true armorbearer—faithful and obedient, even to the point of withstanding Saul's harsh treatment and murderous threats. Because of this attitude, David earned a promotion, to a place of high respect and honor.

Falling on Your Sword

Let's look at another story of Saul and another armorbearer. First Samuel 31:4-6 and 1 Chronicles 10:45 describes another war. Saul and his army were fighting against the Philistines and losing. After Saul's army saw it had no chance of winning the battle, the men turned to flee. Meanwhile, after Saul's sons and men died, the Philistines' arrows wounded him.

In 1 Samuel 31:4 Saul turned to his armorbearer and said, "'Draw your sword and run me through, or these uncircumcised fellows will come and run me through and abuse me.'" Saul asked his armorbearer to kill him, a fate preferable to capture and torture at the hands of the enemy. However, his armorbearer refused to do it, so Saul took his own life by falling on his sword. When his armorbearer saw the king was dead, he too fell on his sword and died.

How many of you would have done that? Would you have the courage to die alongside your leader? Or would you have said something like, "Oh my goodness, how am I going to tell the church members that our leader is dead? How can I make it back myself without getting captured and tortured?"

Have you ever seen the movie *Dave*? When the lead character became president of the United States, his driver and servant told the president that he would take a bullet for him. Now why is it that our government exhibits such commitment, but in the Kingdom of God, you're on your own? It's as if someone says, "I'm with you all the way—unless all hell breaks loose."

Saul's armorbearer stood strong with him, to the very end, as seen by one other noteworthy element of this story. When Saul's sons and his men died, and Saul was wounded, his armorbearer remained upright. His armorbearer had to be in close proximity for Saul to ask him to slay the king, yet there is no mention that the armorbearer suffered any wounds. The practical lesson for today is that God will keep you safe from harm when you obey Him and remain faithful and loyal to your pastor. You can never go wrong when you're faithful.

> *Jeremiah 7:23 "But I gave them this command: Obey me, and I will be your God and you will be my people. Walk in all the ways I command you, that it may go well with you."*

Another point in this story is where we read that when Saul's army saw that defeat was imminent, they ran. Notice who was right there with him when everyone else fled or was killed? His armorbearer. The lesson for all armorbearers is to stay with your pastor, even when times get hard. Anybody can stand by when everything is going well. God is looking for those who have the courage to stand and be counted when the chips are down.

I believe that every pastor needs an armorbearer— someone to act as his or her eyes and ears, and cover him or her in prayer daily. Pastors are looking for someone who they can count on and trust, even in the hard times. Someone they can be themselves with, without fearing they will lose their respect.

When describing pastors, I like the analogy of "Superman" and "Clark Kent." Superman is the persona who shows up in the pulpit. But the one who shows up in the office Monday through Friday, the one who is having a bad day, who just walked past you without speaking, who sometimes gets moody, is Clark Kent. Many pastors get burned out so quickly because they have to stay in their Superman suit. They can't come down from the mountain. They can't let the staff or their armorbearer see their nakedness because if they do, they will lose their respect. How sad! What a shame!

Yet, when leaders fall, we shake our heads at them in disbelief, embarrassment, shame, or disgust. I would ask: Were you there to hold his or her arms up? Were you there to reassure that all would be well or did you leave him or her out to dry? How many pastors are left alone, deserted and vulnerable? Were you praying for him or her? Armorbearers, where are you? Are you in hiding? Why? It's time to come out. Our pastors need us.

Study Questions

1. Have you lost your joy? If so, what steps are you taking to recover it?

_____

_____

_____

_____

_____

_____

2. How can you keep your leader focused on his or her assignment?

_____

_____

_____
_____
_____
_____

3. When you die, will it matter that you were even born? Why?

_____
_____
_____
_____
_____

4. What do you see as the armorbearer's most important roles?

_____
_____
_____
_____
_____

5. Do you feel needed by your leader? Why?

_____
_____
_____
_____
_____

6. What have you said or done to let your leader know that you can be trusted?

_____

_____

_____

_____

_____

_____

7. What can you do to create an atmosphere to make your leader feel relaxed and comfortable?

_____

_____

_____

_____

_____

_____

Chapter 2

Are You an Armorbearer or a Pallbearer?

Flashbulbs popped as we stepped out of the car, a sea of arms stretching across the sidewalk amid a chorus of calls: "Man of God! How are you, brother? Great to see you!" Reporters' microphones extended through the crowd. Excitement filled the air. My head swam at the attention, even though I knew it wasn't directed at me. As I mentioned earlier, when I first started serving my pastor in the late 1980's, I never dreamed a church of a few hundred people could grow to such proportions.

The above scene may sound more like a greeting for a movie star, athlete, or political dignitary, but in today's world many pastors are receiving such accolades. I have been part of more than one ministry whose conferences attract crowds numbering in the thousands. Visitors get packed so tightly in some venues that they turn into mobs of pushing, pulling, and shoving bodies, forcing me to reach out to protect my pastor from harm.

However, acting as an armorbearer only means brief flashes in the limelight. Service is a calling that entails much more. It means giving life and support. During my first ten years of working with my pastor, I knew I was in the right place at the right time. My presence brought him joy and strength, which are among the armorbearer's essential tasks.

So is maintaining a spirit of discernment. I carefully selected when and where to approach him. There were times when he was in fellowship with God and I had to remain quiet. There were also times when we read the same books so we could discuss them later, or shared insights about particular Bible passages. On some occasions we swapped jokes or talked about private matters that only we knew about and promised not to reveal to anyone else. We also called each other daily, including when I went on vacation. At some point of the day, I checked in just to make sure everything was well with him.

However, as the years passed, the glow of service faded. Instead of looks of joy, I often wore a sad countenance. I no longer enjoyed spending time with him or our conversations. My hopes and dreams were fading. Since I found little joy in serving, I had little strength left to impart. Instead of giving life to my leader, I was sucking it out of him. Instead of an armorbearer, I had turned into a pallbearer.

What's the difference? An armorbearer helps carry and protect his leader and assures his or her safety. The armorbearer brings and speaks life. A pallbearer likes to carry dead things around, carefully protecting them so no one can get close or touch them. Pallbearers speak words that lack life; they are full of doom and gloom. I have attended funerals where there weren't enough pallbearers, so they pulled someone out of the audience to help carry the casket. You can't just summon anyone to be an armorbearer, though. They are carefully selected.

As an armorbearer, you must always remain sensitive to timing and God's voice. Know when the brook has dried up and recognize when His provision is moving in your life. How can you tell if you're an armorbearer or a pallbearer? If your leader frowns when you walk into the room, you are headed in the wrong direction. Is your leader happy to see you arrive or more pleased when you leave the room? If the pastor is troubled, does he or she still seek your presence and want your advice? If not, you may want to try on a pair of white gloves. You are becoming a pallbearer instead of a life-giving armorbearer.

Growing Spiritually

As I mentioned in chapter 1, I knew God had called me to serve my former pastor. I knew that one of my purposes for being on this earth was to serve pastors. During my time with him, I served a host of other pastors and leaders, including acting as their designated driver. Because they trusted him and he trusted me, they trusted me. They knew I would help them feel secure and safe without fear of exposure or destructive gossip.

During those early years, though I had no idea what it would eventually take to function in that position, I knew that God had called me to it. However, one of the mistakes I made in those early days was thinking I could serve a noted spiritual leader without being expected to grow spiritually. I thought I could sit under his anointing, yet not be expected to change or mature. As long as he was growing in his teaching and preaching, that would be fine. However, as he grew, I realized I too had to grow in order to stay abreast of his views, thoughts, needs, and ideas. In the same way, other armorbearers must grow spiritually alongside their pastor. You too will be stretched and tested. Why? Because God has a plan for your life.

Another mistake I made was thinking I wouldn't experience any hurt, pain, rejection, or mistreatment because I was serving a man of God. I reasoned that I worked for the church, a respected institution, so I wouldn't face criticism. Wrong! I experienced a multitude of challenges that I was not prepared to face. Needless to say, I ended up disillusioned and upset with myself and my pastor. I saw that the servant's role is not just giving a leader a glass of water, a change of clothes, and carrying his or her books. It will cost your life because it includes dying to self. It will prompt you to pray in the middle of the night for your leader, even when you are dog-tired. It will attract ridicule and such derogatory names as "flunky," "doormat," "gofer," "slave," or "Uncle Tom." In spite of the hurt and loneliness, you must be faithful and always continue to serve with joy.

I recall in my earlier years of serving when I was going through such tough and difficult times that I sometimes daydreamed of committing suicide. The weight of everything I dealt with wore me down. Not understanding what comes with the territory, I didn't have enough maturity to ignore what people were saying about me. I didn't understand that sometimes I would carry some of my pastor's weight. I didn't know that sometimes I would feel his pain because I would hear what the people were saying about him and see how that affected him.

I thought I could just go to church, do whatever was asked of me, and then go home. Instead, I found myself facing a mountain of tasks. As the church grew, I had to be on hand for three Sunday services,

Wednesday night services, attending and planning events during the week, and traveling with my pastor. I walked the halls, greeted people before and after services, and put on a smile when I didn't feel like smiling. I wanted to carry as much of his load as possible so he could stay focused on his assignment.

Not long after I told my pastor in the hospital, "Helping you is killing me," I heard the Holy Spirit whisper, "That's what I'm trying to do...kill you." It was like a spiritual slap in the face. Instantly I remember what Jesus said in Matthew 10:39, "Whoever finds his life will lose it, and whoever loses his life for my sake will find it." How casually we can treat those words, until we have to carry them out! Through this agonizing lesson, I learned that not only will he who loses his life gain it, but he who tries to save his life will lose it. I had to learn to trust God and stop trying to please men. I had to stop trying to rely on my strength and start trusting the "I AM" who created the world.

Being a servant means to give away your life, although it doesn't mean that you have no life. However, your first and highest call is remaining faithful with those tasks God has given us to do. Sadly, we live in the kind of world where few people are willing to give their lives away. The armorbearer stands in direct contrast to this trend, for he or she is willing to give away his or her life.

There is a distinct difference between being an assistant and an armorbearer. You can assist someone without dying to self and without even knowing that person. But you cannot serve someone until you have given your dreams, hopes, and aspirations to God and trusted that He will bring them to pass as you are faithful in serving another's dream. You cannot serve until you want what they want to come to pass.

You may ask, "What about my dreams? What about what I want? What about what God has promised me? Do I just pretend that God hasn't given me gifts and talents to use for His glory?" No. Trust God to bring those things to pass while you are faithfully serving another man or woman. It may sound crazy, but I can honestly say that when I began to faithfully serve my pastor without fear of what people thought or said, I received overwhelming blessings. I saw and experienced things and received blessings that, at the time, I had no way of paying for or accomplishing myself. I traveled to places that in the past I only dreamed of visiting. God will always bless the faithful!

Spiritual Supporter

One primary reason pastors quit, grow weary, or die early is because they don't have prayed-up men and women surrounding them. Too many would-be armorbearers today are searching for glamour and fame; they want the "bling bling." Such striving misses the purpose of their call.

Does this mean all the weight should be placed on the armorbearer without leaders taking responsibility for their actions? Absolutely not! Still, pastors need secure men and women around them. They need people who are "prayed up" and can offer sound advice. They need people who believe in and practice fasting. Trusted armorbearers are those who believe in going the extra mile to insure their leader's success and safety.

That is why you need a clear, convincing call from God to serve your pastor. Some people can't handle knowing the good, the bad, and the ugly. If they see their pastor as transparent, vulnerable, and human, it makes it too difficult to receive from them when they are in the pulpit and the rest of the world looks on them as "Superman."

Approximately ten years into my twelve-year term of service with my former pastor, loneliness and isolation began marking my life. This turned into a huge challenge. I liked being free and socializing with other people. I found myself so lonely that I started griping to myself, "Pastor, you are not going to monopolize my time. I have a life of my own. I have served you for years and now it's my time." This bad attitude was solely of my own making. Had I expressed my thoughts, I would have discovered my pastor was willing to give me the space I needed.

This failure to communicate cost me dearly. I remember a time when several people in the church sought to befriend me. My pastor expressed displeasure. Not because he didn't want me to have any friends, but because he wisely sensed that their motives were not pure. Undeterred, I plunged ahead, developing what I thought were close friendships. After all, I needed some social outlets. To this day, I regret some of those decisions. My pastor was correct. Many were fair-weather friends with ulterior motives and agendas.

I wanted to do my own thing without my pastor's counsel, free from the stress of ministry. Likewise, if you are associating with people and your pastor is not pleased with those relationships, you may want to discuss the reasons. If he or she feels uneasy about your friendships, nine times out of ten, your pastor is likely to question you and your motives. Avoid any relationships that will cause such divisions.

As his aide and spiritual supporter, you have an obligation from God to see to your pastor's safety. If you believe him or her to be a prophet and filled with discernment, trust such judgment. I know you want your freedom and friends outside of church. I did too. When I turned this concern over to God, He sent me real friends who didn't have ulterior motives and liked me for me. They believe in God, they understand serving and we maintain our friendships to this day.

Paying Close Attention

Over the years I have been blessed to oversee several churches' administrative staffs. One thing I advise people is to never enter their pastor's presence without paper and pen. Never attend church without your Bible, paper, and pen because you never know when he or she will give instructions or nuggets of wisdom. Make sure that you pay close attention to what your pastor is saying from the pulpit. Servants have to remain watchful and focused on their leader.

Don't get so caught up on point A that you miss point B.

The first question you need to ask yourself is: Has God called me to serve this man or woman? If the answer is yes, then the next question you need to ask is: What is it that God wants me to do in serving His leader? Why is that so important? Each pastor is different. I have served several and what God told me to do for one pastor, He didn't tell me to do for the next. Their visions and needs were different.

Remember that your call to serve extends to your pastor's family. Never proclaim that you are called to serve your leader but can ignore his or her spouse and children. If you are called to serve the pastor, you are called to serve the family too. It is like a marriage. You didn't just marry your spouse; you married the whole family. When I see servants ignore their leader's spouse, I say to myself, "That's a hireling. That is definitely trouble. This person is not an armorbearer. They have some kind of agenda."

Yet, even as you seek to serve your pastor and family, you must avoid getting too familiar with your pastor. We can become so familiar with our leaders that we begin to devalue them and treat them as common. Familiarity is an evil spirit that strategically infiltrates individuals, families, and churches. Familiarity robs from us what God wants to do in and through us. Familiarity doesn't take something away from us because that would be too obvious. Instead, it simply redefines what we have, causing us to devalue that thing or person. Remember to respect the office that they hold.

Be especially mindful that there is a thin line that every armorbearer must be careful not to cross. Because God has called you to serve His servant leader, you will establish a close relationship. Be careful it isn't so familiar you start to look down on your leader. When I made this mistake, I knew it was time for me to leave that ministry. I'm not saying that you can't have a close relationship with your pastor, but be careful to not get it out of order or twisted. God called you to serve, not to be "buddy buddy." If the two of you can handle that, so be it, but be extremely careful about this situation. It may come back to bite you later.

A familiar spirit will cause you to add "but" after every miracle and blessing of God. This is demonstrated by Matthew 13:54-56: "Coming to his hometown, he began teaching the people in their synagogue, and they were amazed. 'Where did this man get this wisdom and these miraculous powers?' they asked. 'Isn't this the carpenter's son? Isn't his mother's name Mary, and aren't his brothers James, Joseph, Simon and Judas? Aren't all his sisters with us? Where then did this man get all these things?'" Though the people were astonished at Jesus' wisdom and teachings, they made wisecracks about His heritage, family lineage, and mother. They were familiar to everyone, so what made this guy so special?

Be careful not to repeat the mistake the people of Nazareth made, as shown in verses 57-58: And they took offense at him. But Jesus said to them, 'Only in his hometown and in his own house is a prophet without honor.' And he did not do many miracles there because of their lack of faith."

God wants to bless you. He wants to perform miracles in your life. A familiar spirit will rob you of wonder and strip you of the faith that accompanies amazement. It caused Christ's contemporaries to look on His flesh while being blinded to his divine nature. As we read in 2 Corinthians 4:7: "But we have this treasure in jars of clay." A familiar spirit will cause you to focus on the jar of clay instead of the treasure, seeing your pastor's weaknesses instead of the man of God that he represents. A familiar spirit will cause you to critique everything your pastor does instead of helping.

Once familiarity sets in, it will cause you to look at a priceless antique and sneer, "It's just an old bowl." It will make you look at your pastor and say, "Well, he's just a man." It will cause you to miss out on your blessings. Familiarity sets in when we have been around something or someone too long. Are you struggling with a spirit of familiarity? You can be free from it. You can dismantle it by having a spirit of gratitude and thankfulness.

Thank God for who He has placed over you. You have been given a gift. Remember the jar of clay and the treasure in it? Your pastor is a treasure. Become enthusiastic about what you do. Be excited that God has called you to serve. Remember, he who is great among you is your servant.

Hungry for Protection

Pastors are hungry for armorbearers. We can look at fallen pastors and leaders in recent times and see that they needed armorbearers. With all that is happening in the world today and pastors being exposed and uncovered, do you think this is a coincidence? No. The devil is out to destroy those who are bringing God's Word, particularly those who have huge followings. If he can bring down the visible, more people may fall by the wayside. However, that does not exclude pastors with smaller ministries. The devil is after them as well.

The blame doesn't fall solely on pastors. Where were the armorbearers who were called to serve them and cover them in prayer? Where were the people who said, "Pastor, I got you covered," or "Pastor, I got your back"? Armorbearers have a responsibility to cover our leaders, protect them, and insure their safety. The devil is out to destroy them.

Pastors especially need protection because they aren't perfect. Too often their flocks maintain that unrealistic expectation. One reason pastors are falling into immorality, quitting the ministry, or "sneaking and peeking" is because there are no armorbearers to love and respect them if the pastors share honest feelings. Many pastors are dying on the inside because they have to constantly maintain perfection. Where is the outlet? Where are those who genuinely care? No one wants to fall into sin, but where can they go to be heard without fear of being exposed?

Look at Samson and Delilah. Why did the world's strongest man get so desperate that he revealed his secret? Was it so bad that he was willing to sleep with the enemy? Was he so blind that he couldn't see what was happening? Or, was he enjoying the game? You can't play the game and expect to win, which Samson's sad tale in Judges 16:10-20 confirms. We rarely accept the fact that the devil is trying to destroy us, our homes, our marriages, our communities, our purpose and our ministries, and uses certain people to accomplish this goal. And yet, pastors are often willing to talk to anyone who will listen because they are desperate for companionship, attention, and respect.

Armorbearers, are you there for your pastor? You have a responsibility to cover your pastor and pray for him or her. Your pastor needs to be covered. The devil is having a field day in destroying our pastors' reputations. Will anybody say, "Enough is enough" and start serving? Somebody has to do it. Will it be you?

I repeat: the time for glamour-seeking assistants has passed. Armorbearers can't just travel with their leaders and not cover them in prayer. Your pastor doesn't just need Bible carriers, towel washers, and water pourers. He needs praying men and women to cover him daily. Are you called to serve your pastor? If the answer is "yes," then drop to your knees and pray for your leader. Your pastor needs you. He needs you to keep a confidence. They need to know that you can be trusted.

I once heard a statement that I have carried with me throughout my career: "Loose lips sink ships." Your pastor has to be able to trust you. Can you be trusted? Sometimes the load may seem too hard to carry, but where are you when he needs to talk? Are you out doing your own thing and leaving him uncovered?

There is a desperate cry for armorbearers today! Armorbearers are to watch and study their leader to see how they respond to certain situations. I recall praying to God in the early 1990s that I wanted to serve my pastor diligently. I asked God to give me his heart and insights into his thoughts so if I were called on to respond in his absence, I would say what he would say. It takes time, and yes, you will make mistakes, but continue to strive. Never give up. Although since called to serve in another ministry, I can sometimes still feel what my former pastor is facing. When I do, I pray and cover him, his family, and his ministry.

Good communication will help you achieve such insights. Communication is a key ingredient to serving your leader. Doors of communication have to remain open in order for you to be successful. Communication goes both ways, from leader to servant and vice versa. I have seen servants get so wrapped up into other matters that they forget to obtain instructions from their leader.

A true armorbearer does not look for recognition or appreciation. Is recognition and appreciation good to receive? Of course, but if you don't receive accolades, don't let a lack of applause hold you back from serving. A true armorbearer does not try to be out front so he or she can be seen. Remember Christ's words: "The greatest among you will be your servant." In most situations, servants have to be as strong, sensitive, and discerning as their leader. I'm not talking about physical strength, but secure within themselves. I'm not talking about being sensitive emotionally, but sensitive to the Holy Spirit.

I often tell people that not everybody can work for the church. Not everybody can handle the behind-the-scenes details and demands of daily ministry life. It takes a special breed of people to work for the church, just as it takes a special person to serve the pastor. Every person that is called to serve in ministry is not called to serve in close proximity of the pastor. Jesus had twelve disciples, but He only chose three to walk closely with Him. Again, you have to know that you know that God has you on that assignment. Your pastor needs to know that you are dependable and reliable. Your pastor is to speak the vision. It is the servant's responsibility to carry out this vision and help it come to pass.

Study Questions

1. In addition to what you read in this chapter, what other ways can someone tell if they are acting as an armorbearer or pallbearer?

_____

_____

_____

_____

_____

_____

2. When you experience hurt, pain and disappointment, how do you relieve it?

_____

_____

_____

_____

_____

_____

3. What steps are you taking to grow spiritually?

_____

_____

_____

_____

4. How can you avoid becoming too familiar with your leader?

_____

_____

_____

_____

_____

5. Does your leader seek your advice, ideas, and suggestions? If so, why? If not, why?

_____

_____

_____
_____
_____
_____

6. Ask yourself, has God called you to serve your leader? How do you know?

_____
_____
_____
_____
_____
_____

7. How do you handle serving your leader's dream, when your own dream has not come to pass?

_____
_____
_____
_____
_____
_____

Chapter 3

In Times of Testing

By all appearances, I was living the good life. I enjoyed first-class travel, luxurious hotel stays, and five-star dining whenever I accompanied my pastor on the road. The fashionable clothing and interesting, urbane people I had the privilege of meeting added spice to my life. Many people looked at me and said, "Man, you are blessed to do what you do. You get to travel with a man of God and experience so many things."

"Well, there have to be some benefits," I used to think. *"If people only knew the demands of all this travel and the spiritual warfare I have to go through! If you are operating in your purpose, you will experience trials and tribulations. I may look great on the outside, but I am dying on the inside. I am lonely, frustrated, and often depressed."*

However, in His unmistakeable style, one day God let me know that none of this mattered. Not the appearances that attracted the envy of onlookers, or the pressures that I thought dogged me day and night.

"This is not about you or your pastor," He said clearly one day as I prayed. "Yes, I have blessed you to do all of these things, meet all these people, and to travel all of these places. But I have a plan and purpose here. It's all about My Kingdom! It's easy to get caught up into the hype. It's easy to get comfortable in those types of settings. If you're not careful, you can get so accustomed to comfort that your prayer life begins to fade away. All is going well for you. You stop fasting as much as you used to because all is going well. You have become lax! I don't just want you fat and happy. I want your obedience."

God has a way of stripping everything and everybody away that you have a tendency to cling to. In the days and weeks after He spoke so bluntly to me, God often led me to Proverbs 3:5-6: "Trust in the Lord with all your heart and lean not on your own understanding; in all your ways acknowledge him, and he will make your paths straight."

I quoted that scripture over and over until I started to believe it. It helped strengthen me. Believe me, you have to be strong and secure to serve. Sometimes, you will have to do what David did in 1 Samuel 30:6 and encourage yourself in the Lord. You may start out on the rough side, but keep pressing, praying, and fasting. Keep striving and seeking God, knowing that along the way you will face tests and trial. Yet, if you want to serve, He will direct your path.

Willing to Serve

Serving is an honor and privilege, but as I've said previously, it's also a daily dying to self. Are you willing to do whatever it takes to serve? We are all called to serve one another, as spelled out in Galatians 5:13: "You, my brothers, were called to be free. But do not use your freedom to indulge the sinful nature; rather, serve one another in love."

The issue you must honestly face is whether you are serving with hidden motives or agendas. Are you secretly seeking glory? Prestige? Status? Always fix your eyes on God, because there will come times when you will want to hurt your pastor. Why? Because it's hard to control the flesh. If you are in service to please other men and women, you won't last.

Be devoted, loyal, committed, faithful, and trust-worthy. Maintain a confidence. If you struggle with keeping your mouth shut or are always murmuring and complaining, don't climb in the ring. If you are the type of person who makes excuses for your actions, don't sign up for action. If you know you are unreliable and can't be trusted, find another place. God is looking for those who are tired of all of the "drama" going on in the church today. He's looking for men and women who have declared, "Come what may, I'm in it for the long haul. I am going to take my rightful position."

Whether board members, trustee committees, church council members, or deacons, for many years I have seen people come and go in churches. I have seen more than once the *appointed* board attempted to kick out the *anointed* man or woman of God. That isn't their purpose or task. If God called these pastors to positions of leadership, He can also remove them without anybody's help. Many people have died prematurely and have even gotten sick because they have put their hands and mouths on the man or woman of God.

As I have already acknowledged, I too have made the mistake of murmuring, complaining, gossiping about, or second-guessing the pastor because things weren't going the way that I wanted them to go. Whenever you reach such a place, it may be time to start packing your bags. You are on dangerous ground. You can't effectively serve and criticize at the same time. It took me years to hear God clearly telling me, "This is My church and man-servant." When I tried to handle the situation myself, all I did was get in the way of what God wanted to accomplish.

An armorbearer can't afford to get sidetracked into griping and complaining against the pastor. Trust is a major factor in a relationship between a pastor and his or her armorbearer. If there is no trust, there will be no success, regardless of how talented an individual. If there is mistrust or feelings of betrayal, you might as well throw in the towel. Unless God intervenes, that relationship will never work.

One of the reasons I think some pastors find it hard to trust their armorbearers is because the servant is trying to become the pastor. Armorbearers must know their place. Know where God has placed you and serve there. We can get mad at the pastor for not trusting us, but some of that is because of the insults they had to endure from other backstabbing, in-house leaders.

The sad truth is the world often laughs at the church when we should be the most united group of people around. Yet, we often have some of the most intense drama going on in our lives, as if we lived in a real-life soap opera. Divorce, domestic violence, adultery, rape, and child molestation are a few of the sad tales. We must stop playing games. God is tired of playing with us. He is no longer tolerating our messes. Instead, He is exposing sin in the camp.

Providing Strength

One of the ways you can tell that your time of serving your pastor is coming to an end is when you enter a room and your presence irritates and annoys him or her. The result is a spirit of gloom. Your presence should bring about peace, joy, and victory. It is an integral part of your purpose and lifestyle. I have observed armorbearers drain their pastors mentally, emotionally, financially, physically, and spiritually. As an armorbearer, you are to provide strength.

If you are not providing that strength and bringing joy into his or her life, you need to sit down with your pastor and ask some serious questions. What was once a God thing can also become dead if you stay longer than what God planned. Take it from me. I stayed in one place too long and became stagnant. Eventually I was in the way of what God wanted to do in that ministry, and what He wanted to do in my life. Timing is crucial. You have to know when it's time to move to the next phase of life.

Automaker and industrial pioneer Henry Ford once said, "Coming together is a beginning. Staying together is progress. Working together is success." Armorbearers, it takes working together if you hope to see success. It takes communication. Can you handle being first at being second? Think about it. True armorbearers do not care who gets the credit. They don't care who is out front. They receive their joy by serving.

A good armorbearer also learns not to hold grudges. After being rejected and wounded by one pastor, when it came time to serve another, I served my new leader based on my past pain and rejection. The moment I saw similar traits, I immediately put up my guard and served half-heartedly. Was it fair to that pastor? Of course not, but I feared facing rejection again. I was afraid of being vulnerable. I would listen to the devil when he whispered, "Remember what happened the last time you served faithfully? Remember the last time when you gave your all and they took advantage of you?"

This is why deliverance and healing from insecurity is so important, as illustrated by 2 Samuel 9:6-8: "When Mephibosheth son of Jonathan, the son of Saul, came to David, he bowed down to pay him honor. David said, 'Mephibosheth!' 'Your servant,' he replied. 'Don't be afraid,' David said to him, 'for I will surely show you kindness for the sake of your father Jonathan. I will restore to you all the land that belonged to your grandfather Saul, and you will always eat at my table.' Mephibosheth bowed down and said, 'What is your servant, that you should notice a dead dog like me?'"

Mephibosheth was so insecure about himself and had such a poor self-image that when David called him to be blessed, he thought he faced rejection and denial. We have some Mephibosheths with the title of armorbearer. Ironically, a poor self-image makes it difficult to serve (or be served.) Seeing yourself in a bad light causes you to operate in a spirit of fear. It could cause you to shy away from what rightfully belongs to you. There are many servants operating in fear, which causes a lack of trust, mistreatment, rejection, and ultimately unfaithfulness to what God has called you to do. It's time to get free!

Listening, Praying & Standing in Faith

Not only must a good armorbearer be confident, he or she must be a good listener. More than once I have faced fatigue and yearned to relax at the end of the day, but I knew my pastor needed my ear. He needed to simply let off some steam rather than solicit my advice. This is where male armorbearers have to learn to practice listening. Most men like to solve problems, so when our pastor tells us about a challenge he is facing, we want to help solve the problem.

Not only do armorbearers need discernment regarding when to offer advice, they have to be extremely careful about the words of wisdom they dispense. If your pastor listens to your input, when he asks you a question, you better be sure that you hear from God. The best way to do that is to be in a constant state of prayer.

A good armorbearer is a prayer warrior, one who knows how to get a prayer through to heaven. He knows how to press through in prayer and not give up. He is discerning and watchful at all times, listening and paying attention to details. An armorbearer is praying for the pastor, his family, the ministry, and its vision. The armorbearer is not wrapped up in his own agendas. He knows that he must pray in order to continue to serve, because serving can make you want to operate in the flesh.

Such a presence of prayer means your leader will feel a sense of peace when you are around. I remember when my former pastor requested to see me quite often. One time I asked, "Why did you need me? He replied, "I needed your presence because I feel at ease or at peace when you are in here." Wow! Talk about a good feeling. Of course, as good as it felt when I would hear him say that he needed my presence, it felt just as bad when he would tell me to get out of his office because my face was getting on his nerves.

The latter is one of the challenges of service, which you will have to work through in order to remain faithful. When I received the first "blow" of hurt, pain, and what I thought to be mistreatment from my pastor, I found that difficult. I didn't want to serve a man who hurt me. However, God kept reminding me that He called me to the assignment, so I had no choice but to be committed. I had to fast, pray, and talk to God daily.

In addition, I read material on serving as if I were a starving man at an all-you-can-eat buffet. That is how I felt about serving. I knew I couldn't quit, so I started cramming reading material into my spirit so that I wouldn't get out of a servanthood position. I knew that the devil was after my calling and having a field day with me, my attitude, and my mind and thinking patterns.

Be aware that when you are hurting and in pain, the devil will use that to throw you off course. He will make you tell yourself things like, "I told you not to trust him. I told you not to serve him because he doesn't care about you. If he did, he wouldn't have done so-and-so." The devil did this to rob me of sleep, a clear mind, and my appetite. I started losing weight and became a prime target for the devil. I had to read, pray, fast, and memorize passages from the Word about serving.

As part of my reading, I read about Jonathan's armorbearer in 1 Samuel 14, where Jonathan ordered his armorbearer to accompany him over to the garrison of the Philistines. Although they were the only two against an entire army, Jonathan's armorbearer obeyed his leader. As I read, I got upset with Jonathan's armorbearer for being so faithful. I wanted to read about someone who felt like I had. As I read, I asked God to search my heart and help me. I didn't want to be stuck in my current state. James 4:2 says we don't *have* because we don't *ask*, so I asked God to help me. I didn't want to be out of His will for my life.

As I was praying that prayer and reading the story, I started seeing what God wanted me to gain from it. Verse 7 is what grabbed me. The faithful armorbearer replied, "Do all that you have in mind. Go ahead; I am with you heart and soul." Talk about humility and faithfulness. A faithful armorbearer is one who wins victories for his leader and slays enemies while his leader gets the glory. In that moment God reminded me that it wasn't about me: "There are souls at stake. There are people dying and you are leaving your leaders out there to get killed and trampled on, all because you have been hurt. You are on an assignment from Me, not from man. Now get up and get to your position."

Remaining Faithful

Such experiences are why I encourage armor-bearers to remain faithful, regardless of what they are facing in life. Times will get hard and yes, you will want to quit, but remain faithful to your calling. If you leave your post, be assured that is when your pastor will get attacked. If he or she falls, your pastor's blood will be on your hands. Make sure that you are not found guilty of going AWOL. Believe me, your pastor needs you.

As you serve, remember that merely showing obedience to God doesn't mean the devil is going to leave you alone. I remember one time when I was contemplating leaving my position. As usual, I wasn't thinking about anyone but myself. It didn't matter to me how my pastor felt or what my spouse thought. I just wanted out. I was tired of my pastor's yo-yo mood swings. I was letting my flesh take control again. After I took some time to collect my thoughts, God revealed that I was being selfish and I was about to step outside of His will for my life. It was three years before He released me from that assignment. During those three years, God tested me to see if I was still going to serve with joy, dedication, and energy.

To my fellow armorbearers, I caution that anything less than full submission is rebellion. And rebellion is where the devil operates. I know how easy it is to fall prey to the spirit of rebellion. As I embraced that yearning for independence, I thought, "I'm tired of people telling me what to do. I want to be my own man. Besides, that pastor puts his pants on the same way I do. He's just a man."

There were so many people coming to me and whispering similar thoughts that I often reacted to my pastor based on what others said. I took on their spirit and mindset. Talk about confusion! Be careful who is speaking into your spirit. Everybody is not happy for you or pleased with where you are. Be secure with yourself and know that you are called to do what you do.

Now that God has healed me, I can tell my story. I can tell other armorbearers that they can serve with joy. You can make it and you're going to make it. You have been called by God. I'm still an armorbearer and yes, I'm serving another pastor faithfully. Is he perfect? No, but neither am I. However, I no longer look at him thinking that he's going to hurt or disappoint me. I understand that I am on an assignment by God. Even if my pastor disappoints or hurts me, I now understand that I have to go talk to him about it. I no longer dwell on it and allow the devil to play with my mind.

In chapter 1, I mentioned a primary challenge in the church today: the independent spirit. It is sprouting like mushrooms in a rain forest. No one wants to die to themselves and few want to serve. I believe that independent churches produce independent spirits. Until you learn to submit to authority, God will never establish you as an authority. Armorbearers must resist the independent spirit, because it can easily interfere with their call to faithful service.

Don't think you won't be tempted in this area. God will test you to see if you are going to obey Him or let your flesh remain in control. The more I tried to fight what God was trying to do in me, the longer I had to stay where I was until I passed the test. Ironically, this was the same pastor I thoroughly enjoyed serving a few years earlier. "What changed?" I asked myself one day. "Was it me or him? I know that God didn't change, so who was it?"

I didn't change my mentality or perspective of my pastor when God changed him. I was used to the old man of God. When God started doing new things through him, I had to change my outlook and mindset about him. I was used to serving him on a certain level, but God had moved him up a notch. Many times we get used to seeing a pastor on one level and when God elevates him to another, we don't make the necessary changes. This is where communication is so important.

Blessings Come

All armorbearers should want to see their pastors blessed. I have actually spoken with armorbearers who had a problem seeing their pastors driving a certain make and model car, living in an upscale neighborhood, wearing nice clothes, or flying their own airplane. Granted, there is often a fine line between necessity and luxury, but let me remind you that such patriarchs as Abraham, David, Solomon, and Job were also wealthy. If athletes and the CEO's of major corporations can have such possessions, why can't the man of God who is bringing a Word from God?

Lest you get caught up in envy, experience has shown me that when an armorbearer can't stand to see his or her leader blessed, nine times out of ten the armorbearer won't get blessed either. It brings me joy to serve a blessed man or woman of God. I have come to realize that as he or she is blessed, mine is on the way. Every armorbearer should be excited about the fact that their pastor is blessed and highly favored, just as every pastor should want to see his armorbearer blessed. Who wants to be around cursed people, or someone who is constantly struggling and spreading negativity and doubt? Blessings come from obedience. Get in your position and watch God bless you! Can you stand to be blessed?

Study Questions

1. What are some ways that you can stay focused on your assignment?

_____

_____

_____

_____

_____

_____

2. Have you ever felt like quitting or throwing in the towel? What kept you going?

_____

_____

_____

_____

_____

_____

3. What scripture(s) do you read and meditate on to keep you focused on your assignment? How are they of help?

_____

_____

_____

_____

_____

4. Ask those around you if they view you as a team player? What responses did you receive?

_____

_____

_____

_____

_____

5. Discuss how Jonathon's and David's relationship ultimately blessed Mephibosheth. Then discuss how serving can bless you and your family.

_____

_____

_____

_____

_____

_____

6. Read Galatians 5:13 on serving. How do you seek to fulfill this verse? Discuss this further with members of your study group.

_____

_____

_____

_____

_____

_____

Chapter 4

Remain Faithful

When I was called to serve my pastor, I was determined to not let anyone out-serve me as I served him. I knew that if I took good care of the man of God, God would take good care of me. It is similar to what I often tell my wife: "I'm going to make it hard for someone else to come in and take my place. I'm going to treat you so good and set the bar so high that if I die before you and you remarry, the next man better bring his A game."

The body of Christ should act the same way. Each of us should be known for his or her "serve-ability," even if it rubs others the wrong way. I recall when I gave the staff orders to clean the pastor's car each week, pick up his clothes from the cleaners, and take care of other small tasks so he could remain focused on his assignment. People were not thrilled with these ideas, complaining I was putting him on a pedestal. I didn't want these things done because he couldn't wash his own car, go to the cleaners, or handle some other tasks. I just felt that if he had fewer things to worry about, the more he could study and be prepared when it was time for him to deliver the Word. My assignment was to make sure that he had ample time to prepare. Souls were at stake.

Despite these attempts to serve wholeheartedly, I hit some bumps along the way. When I discovered that my former pastor had not always been candid with me about a few matters I had asked him about, I was devastated. I would have done anything for him. So when he demonstrated a lack of trust in me it disturbed me. I held on to that hurt and pain for many years, which sometimes hindered my effectiveness in serving. But I kept hearing God say, "Remain faithful."

Even after I resigned from that ministry, I struggled to let go. When God called me to serve elsewhere, it was a struggle. I feared being treated in a similar fashion by another pastor. Believing I would be mistreated, I guarded my heart to protect myself. (By the way, you do know that self-protection is not of God? God told us to trust in Him; self-protection is a sign that you don't. It's like telling God, "I don't believe that You can protect me from this pain, so I'm going to handle it myself.")

No matter what happens, serve your pastor with joy, humility, diligence, and faithfulness, understanding that serving is a privilege that God has given you. Armorbearers are needed so the church can function and the gospel can go forth. Many pastors are experiencing burnout because they have to carry too much unnecessary weight, which burdens them and causes them to lose focus.

Our cities and communities are dying because our pastors cannot break through and take the Word of God to a lost and dying world. Instead, they are patching up too many wounds of soldiers in the camp. Meanwhile, the devil is having a field day. We all have a part in God's Kingdom. There is one body, but different parts of the body have different functions. Armorbearers, know your place. You have been gifted to do what you do. No one else can be you.

Second Corinthians 5:10 says, "For we must all appear before the judgment seat of Christ, that each one may receive what is due him for the things done while in the body, whether good or bad." In other words, each of us has a purpose for being on this earth and in the ministry where we serve. It isn't an accident that you happen to be placed in the city where you live and under the leadership God has placed over you. There are many churches you could attend, but God called you to serve the one where you are.

Since you are in that church, you might as well be faithful. You have a choice in the matter if you want to be blessed. If you are going to complain, murmur, and tear down the ministry, it would be best for you to leave so that God can place His man or woman there. You could be standing in the way of what God wants to do in that ministry. Furthermore, you could be holding up your own blessing.

Be a Blessed Human Being

Strive to be like the man described in Psalms 1:1: "Blessed is the man who does not walk in the counsel of the wicked or stand in the way of sinners or sit in the seat of mockers." Verses 2-3 go on to say, "But his delight is in the law of the Lord, and on his law he meditates day and night. He is like a tree planted by streams of water, which yields its fruit in season and whose leaf does not wither. Whatever he does prospers."

Be like the tree planted by streams of water. That tree will always be fresh, green, and prosperous because it knows its place. You have to know that destination where God has planted you. If you want to prosper, get in your place. If you want to see God move in your life and in the ministry where you serve, get in your place. If you want your dreams and desires to come to pass, get in your place. You have to understand that God has planted each of us in a particular spot.

I once heard someone say, "Trees just don't get up and move. You don't look out your window one day and see that a tree has been moved from one corner to the next." That is true. They are planted. And once they are, they are usually there for a long time. If a tree is uprooted too often, it will eventually die. Its roots become too weak. Have you become weak? Is it because you have been uprooted too many times because someone offended you?

Did you notice the reference in the second half of Psalms 1:3 to bringing forth fruit "in due season"? Have you ever wondered why no fruit is being produced in your life? Check yourself. Inspect your roots. Have you become weak? Too often, armor-bearers get offended, hurt, and rejected and decide to leave their posts when God didn't tell them to go.

In turn, they uproot themselves from the place where God planted them. I have discovered a host of armorbearers who go AWOL because things didn't go their way. Even though they have taken on the role of a servant, they refuse to submit to authority. Just because you have special gifts and talents, it doesn't mean you no longer have to obey your authority. If you don't, you are in rebellion, which is comparable to witchcraft. It is scary to consider that some ministries have been birthed out of rebellion, yet the leaders call it a move of God.

Be careful not to get twisted up in an unhealthy situation, because operating in this type of behavior will keep you from accomplishing all that God wants you to accomplish. The devil has tricked so many people and caused them to uproot themselves, only to find out that they become weak and ineffective. Their countenance changes, their posture slumps, their demeanor grows cloudy, and their conversation becomes negatively charged. What happened? Who tricked them? Who has been talking to them?

If you recognize this kind of situation surrounding your life, realize that the devil is after your calling and servant spirit. He knows you get joy from serving and that you are operating in your purpose. How can you serve effectively when you are weak? How can you serve when you have no joy? The Bible says that the joy of the Lord is our strength.

Playing for the Team

While I'm not a skilled athlete, I know a few things about sports. In football there are owners and general managers who sit up high in the press box. They can see the entire playing field. From their perch they can see who is talking to whom and design strategies to employ against the opposing team. They are calling the plays. In my analogy, God is the one sitting in the press box, calling the shots. He sees everything.

Then we have the head coach, who has a direct line to his assistants in the press box. He stands on the playing field, guiding the quarterback by calling plays. The coach's main purpose is to communicate the plays to the quarterback so the team can win the game. He is also present to encourage and motivate them. The coach never leaves the field, not even in the midst of a horrendous loss. In the church we call our coach the Holy Spirit. He will never leave us or forsake us, always standing with us through the tough times. If you listen to the Holy Spirit, you will win the game.

Then we have the quarterback, whose main purpose is to communicate the coach's directions to the team. If you have an attentive quarterback, you will win. The quarterback cannot be cocky, but must be strong and knowledgeable. In the church, we call him "Pastor." The pastor must listen to the Holy Spirit in order to win the game. I rarely see the quarterback running the ball, unless he has no choice. Players must protect the quarterback because if he gets hurt, it will affect the entire team.

Notice that there are not too many quarterbacks on the team. They are outnumbered by the other players. Everybody can't be the quarterback. Somebody has got to block for him and somebody has got to run the ball. Everyone has to know his role in executing the plays. Only certain players can run down the field and score, or catch long scoring passes. Except for trick plays, only the quarterback can throw those passes.

Amorbearer, don't get upset with your pastor when he seems to always be passing the ball to someone else or giving all of his time and attention to other players on the team. If you can't catch the ball and run with it for a touchdown, why would he pass it to you? Why waste time when you are not paying attention? Or when you are walking around with an attitude? When your countenance is sad and your conversation is negative, why should the pastor waste his or her time with you?

Say the quarterback calls the play and tells the runner to take two steps to the right, then turn left and sprint up the field twenty yards, turn around and the ball will be right there. All the runner has to do is what the quarterback says. But instead, you run, murmur and complain. You've lost count and gotten distracted. Therefore, the runner disobeys the call and, when the ball is thrown, he misses it because he isn't in his place.

The same applies to your calling. Do you want to win the game? Get into your place. God has communicated to the Holy Spirit and the Holy Spirit has communicated to the quarterback. He has told the quarterback to tell you to do this and that, but instead of being obedient, you do your own thing, miss the ball, and the team loses. He has told you to serve with joy, commitment, enthusiasm and dedication and when it's time, turn around and your blessing will be right there. Just do what he tells you. Instead, too often church members get offended along the way. They don't like the play that is called, so they complain to the naysayers and nitpickers. God throws them the pass, but they miss their blessing because they were not in their place. Even worse, they have left the field.

You may have gotten deceived into thinking you should do your own thing. Maybe you allowed someone to tell you that you should go to this church or that ministry. What you failed to realize is that God has been throwing the passes at your former place, but the ball is falling to the ground. Or, someone else is catching all of your blessings because they are planted in your place. It might even be the person who told you to leave. Watch out for those who say they are your friends. They may just want your blessings.

The Armorbearer's purpose

Let's recap some of the armorbearer's purposes:

1. **An armorbearer must be mature.**

He or she cannot be a babe in Christ. When the storms come (and they will come), the servant's responsibility is to encourage the leader. Reassure them that all is well. Let them know that you are with them in the midst of the battle. Be ready to be on the front lines in the midst of adversity, ready to take the bullet or face the enemy's attacks, be that criticisms, complaints, or sarcasm.

2. **An armorbearer helps carry the burden.**

You are an extra set of shoulders for your pastor. As I said in chapter 2, you must be careful to not get too close or so familiar with your leader that you fail to recognize the sovereignty, favor, and anointing that rests on them.

3. **As you pray and seek the Lord about what it is He would have you do for your pastor, be prepared to engage in serious warfare.**

Why do I say this? Because the devil does not like the fact that you are stepping up to the plate to take care of God's man or woman. He gets joy by seeing the body of Christ divided. The devil knows that whenever there is peace and unity, we win.

4. **An armorbearer should be devoted, loyal and committed.**

God is looking for men and women who have said, "Come what may, I'm in it for the long haul. I am going to take my rightful position. I am here to serve and protect God's servant."

5. **Trust is a major factor in a relationship between a pastor and his armorbearer. If there is no trust, there will be no success.**

Regardless of how talented an individual may be, if there is mistrust or feelings of betrayal, you might as well throw in the towel on that relationship. Unless God intervenes, it will never work. An armorbearer must stay in his place of service, where God has placed him.

6. **A good armorbearer is a prayer warrior.**

As I mentioned earlier, being an armorbearer is more than just carrying a Bible, pouring water, or serving as a chauffeur. An armorbearer is a prayer warrior. He or she knows how to press through in prayer and not give up. They are discerning and watchful at all times, listening, and paying attention to details. He is praying for the pastor, his family, the ministry, and the vision, and avoiding getting wrapped up in his own agendas. He knows that he must pray in order to continue to serve.

7.   An amorbearer must remain faithful.

This was a challenge for me. When I received the first "blow" of my pastor's mistreatment. I found it hard to remain faithful. I didn't want to serve a man who hurt me. However, God kept reminding me that I was called to the assignment. I had no choice but to be faithful and committed. I had to fast, pray, and talk to God like never before.

During these times, the Lord reminded me that it wasn't about me—there were souls at stake. There were people dying and I wanted to leave my leader to get trampled on and maybe even killed, all because I felt hurt. He concluded, "You are on an assignment from God, not from man. Now get up and get to your position."

The armorbearer's family

Many armorbearers get caught up in serving their leader and fail to realize that their first church is their home. You can't effectively serve your leader when your own house is going to hell in a handbasket. You can't effectively serve your leader when you are constantly battling with your spouse and your kids don't respect you. People would see my pastor, his family, and me but my wife and kids were oftentimes left alone in the background. Who was protecting them? I am the leader in my home, but who was leading them while I was out serving the man of God?

Many times it was difficult because I knew that I had this calling on my life to serve this world-renowned pastor. Yet, at the same time, I had a wife who was looking for her husband and children who were looking for their father. I was often torn and unsure of what to do. "Lord, do I go and serve my pastor who is depending on me and waiting on me to take my position as an armorbearer?" I would ask. "Or, do I ignore him and go and be the husband to my wife and father to my children who are waiting on me?" Many times, I didn't know what to do; I often made the wrong decision. Still, I took each situation as it came and prayed that I would make the right one.

Although I communicated to my wife what my calling was, there were times that she still wanted her personal pastor—me. I had to also communicate to my pastor that although I may be getting an "A" with him, I was getting an "F" at home and was in danger of losing my family. Because he cared for me and my well being, he would often say, "Go, be with your family. They need you."

Although he would release me to go see about my family and be with my family, I would still feel guilty because I left my post, leaving him uncovered. However, if I stayed with him, I would feel guilty for not going to my family, leaving them uncovered.

Talk about inner turmoil and drama. I would often ask God, "Who is serving the armorbearer? Lord, do you care about me? Who is looking out for me? Who sees my needs? Lord, help me! I'm losing my mind."

I didn't want my wife or children to resent me or the ministry. Nor did I want God to remove His hand from my life for not operating in my calling. So I asked Him, "God, what do You want from me? What am I supposed to do in this situation?" It was then when I realized that I although I had become a good armorbearer, I was a poor husband and father. When I realized what I had become, I felt like a loser. All the while that I didn't want my family to resent the ministry, I was beginning to resent it myself.

Turned around, I started leaving all of my work at work. When I was home, I was at home with my family. I turned the phone and pager off and gave some quality time to my family. I am the pastor in my house and have four members (none of them tithe, but nevertheless, they are my members). After I turned off all communication devices so that I could spend some quality time with my family, my wife didn't mind me serving my pastor whole-heartedly. She just needed her time. My children didn't mind if I had to travel and be away from home. They just wanted some daddy time.

If we are not careful, we can allow the ministry to kill and destroy us and our families. I was eating and drinking "ministry." All I thought about was serving. Yet I was losing my family at the same time. I didn't know how to balance the two. I knew that somebody was going to be unhappy. I would either leave my wife or pastor uncovered. Never mind how I felt; I was trying to please everyone else. The key question here is: What good does it do you if you serve your pastor and his family with joy and excellence and lose your own family? Well, that's the road I was on—one that ends in divorce. My wife was becoming fed up with me and the ministry. All along, I knew that God had called me to serve my pastor, but I also knew that He had given me my wife.

My wife had dreams and desires of her own that she wanted to accomplish. I knew that if she was working outside the home, there was a good chance that I wouldn't have the support and encouragement I needed to accomplish my purpose. Therefore, she decided to be a stay-at-home mom to raise our children. I know that a pastor's family goes through a lot, but if you are a good armorbearer, your family will make sacrifices as well because you have no life. Your life becomes ministry. Your life no longer belongs to you.

Armorbearers, take care of your family. If you don't, the devil will be waiting so that he can destroy them. Learn to balance your calling and purpose. Yes, God called you to serve, but not at the expense of losing your family. I probably would have never changed until the pain of not changing became greater than the pain of change. Don't wait until it's too late to make the necessary changes to save your family. Start now! Your life does matter. You are needed.

By Kateena Gates

As the wife of an armorbearer, my call is both a blessing and a sacrifice. The blessing is to have a husband with a servant's heart who does not mind dying to himself, knows his purpose, and hears from God. My family is blessed because of the many sacrifices that he makes for me and our children.

As the armorbearer's wife, I am called to be his armorbearer. In the beginning of his ministry to our pastor, I didn't quite understand his role, not to mention my role as his wife. I would often hear him say that he was called to be the eyes and ears for the pastor, an encourager, and one who was to hold up the pastor's arms and make sure his needs were met.

His mind was constantly on serving. When we attended church services, I knew that he was going to be "tuned in" to the pastor. Therefore, I had to keep my eyes and ears open to watch his back and make sure that he, too, was covered in prayer. Because he is so dedicated to his God-given assignment, I knew that I had to learn the importance of watching, praying, and listening.

We went through some difficult times in the early years of ministry because I knew God's order: after Him, I came next. However, there were times when I didn't feel that way—mainly because I didn't understand, although a lot of it had to do with him getting his priorities out of order. Still, over time I learned by watching him serve. While he is watching the pastor, I am watching and covering him. My role is to pray and intercede for my husband.

I am constantly asking God to keep him focused on his assignment and to give him clear direction, make Everett sensitive to His voice, and give him a strong spirit of discernment. Yes, I am sensitive to his physical needs, but it is just as important to be sensitive to his spiritual needs. An armorbearer's spouse needs to be sensitive and attentive to servants needs. I ask God to connect us in such a way that his needs are met before he even has to ask. If he is in need of intercessory prayer for a particular situation, I pray for that on his behalf.

As individuals we often can be selfish in our attitude towards serving. But as was mentioned earlier in the book, we have allowed the devil to destroy ministries, homes, marriages, relationships and communities because of this selfish mentality. I would often see my husband taking such good care of the man of God that I would tell myself, "I need to make sure that I am taking good care of him." I learned by watching him that blessings come from dying to yourself and serving.

For example, in ministry he is required to wear a certain type of clothing to certain type of events, services, and conferences. It is my job to stay current with his needs for clothing and shoes, so I would go and purchase what he would need before he has to ask (not that I mind shopping.) When I notice that he hasn't eaten properly for several days, it is my job to provide healthy meals.

My husband's expectations are minimal when he is at church. It is during that time that he is looking to me for support and understanding. Once church is over, my expectations increase. This is where the sacrifice comes in, when the ministry's needs, demands, and telephone calls seem to interfere with family time. So that our children won't despise ministry, my role as the armorbearer's wife is to insure balance. Without this balance, his mind will never shut off from ministry. When that happens, challenges and problems occur within the home.

Balancing my husband's calling and purpose with family life is crucial. Imbalances can be detrimental. During these times I have fought battles, trying to improvise and keep the children busy so they don't notice he is gone. That worked well when the children were younger. Now that they are older it doesn't work as much. This is when communication between my husband and I is extremely important. Communication is the key to any success.

I am not a "yes" wife—I'll just say that I don't cut him much slack. Yes, I will pray, cover, and serve him, but when it is time to shut all that off and just be family, I am expecting him to do the same. That means he is expected to get into my world or the children's world. He is expected to play ball, video games, and attend our son's sports activities. He is expected to shop with and for the girls, date them, and spend quality time with them. He is expected to be my husband, lover, and friend. I expect to be able to go to him before anyone else and share my dreams and desires. Mind you, although these are our expectations it doesn't always go this way, but we strive daily to make it work.

There have been times when these expectations have gone unmet a little too long. The end result has been the question of whether or not he needs to answer this call alone. But I have learned over the years that the easiest way to be an armorbearer's wife is to learn to appreciate each other for who we are, accept the other person's call and personality, and know that God has a call on each of you. He has joined the two of you together to bring it all to pass so that souls can be won for God's Kingdom. God has a call for you as an individual and both of you as a unit.

Study Questions

1. How do you balance family and ministry?

_____

_____

_____

_____

_____

_____

2. Have you ever been found guilty of murmuring or complaining? If so, what steps did you take to repent and embrace a new attitude?

_____

_____

_____

_____

_____

_____

3. List some ways that you can make your family feel comfortable and secure with your calling.

_____

_____

_____

_____

_____

4. What can you do to let your leader know that you are a team player?

_____

_____

_____

_____

_____

5. Have you been healed and delivered from past pain and hurt? If so, how do you know?

_____

_____

_____

_____

6. What do you do to keep your family first in your life (after God?)

_____

_____

_____

_____

_____

Chapter 5

How to Serve an
Overwhelmed Pastor

If your pastor became overwhelmed with ministry, life's struggles, and situations, how would you handle it? If your pastor became a high profile figure or someone with numerous demands on their time, what would you do? My advice is to allow them to have their space and be themselves. As I mentioned in a previous chapter, our pastors are dying prematurely because they constantly have to wear their "Superman Suit." Many times our leaders are overwhelmed because of the demands that come with the position. Yet, there are many who are overwhelmed because of the demands and immaturity of their armorbearers and/or church leaders.

When my former pastor started receiving the recognition from the local church and on state and national levels too, he didn't know how to respond. Consequently, I found it extremely difficult to serve him because he was in an unfamiliar place. When he demonstrated certain behaviors, my actions were not always "Christlike." I started responding negatively towards him, not understanding that this was all new to him as well. So, if he responded with a short-tempered answer as if I was "working his nerve," I reacted in a similar fashion. Were my actions correct? Of course not! Needless to say, this added more stress to his life. I knew that I was supposed to be supportive in my actions, giving him the room to grasp what God was doing in and through him. He was operating on a new level. But I wanted him to understand what I was going through. Needless to say, I had a lot of growing to do.

It was amazing to see the many phases and stages that God took him through. When the church outgrew the original sanctuary, we built a new, gleaming edifice to house all the souls that flocked to Sunday morning services. We arrived around 5 a.m. to prepare for the 6:30 service. The people would gather in that auditorium, ready to "get their praise on," and hear a message from the Lord. Prior to going into the service, we would gather in his office to pray and ask God for His presence.

During that time, I learned to always ask God for His presence prior to doing anything, regardless of how easy it may have looked. As anyone would feel, nerves and fear gripped him because he didn't want to disappoint God, nor did he want to operate in the flesh. By 6:45 a.m., he walked boldly into the pulpit. After the service, he wanted to greet everyone before going into his office to prepare for the 9:30 service. I could see how drained and worn out he felt just by looking at his sweat-drenched clothing.

After getting him prepared for the next service, we headed downstairs so he could deliver a life-transforming message. There were many Sundays that the messages were totally different from service to service. People were delivered, healed, and set free from bondages and struggles. Again, after the second service, he would shake hands and greet people. There were times that I noticed his exhausted looks and would urge him, "Let's just go to the office. You have one more service to preach." He usually refused; he wanted to speak with members. At times I would get upset because I knew that made my challenge that much tougher. After all, it was my role to keep him pumped up, prayed up, focused, encouraged, and motivated.

By the time we reached the office, he would collapse on the sofa, leaving me to sometimes question God. I would mutter to myself, *How can God do this to anybody?* There were some Sundays that we would have only a half-hour before the last service started. While he had other armorbearers, as his chief armorbearer and the closest person to him, I had the responsibility of deciding who should come into the office. Naturally, I created enemies. Often, when I yielded and let someone come in, many would sit around and stare. I would think, *Stop staring and speak life* or *Stop staring and start praying; give him some encouragement and motivation. Can't you see that he is wiped out?*

Shortly after a few moments of rest, it would be time for the final service and some blessed rest—that is, if I hadn't booked him to speak in the afternoon or fly somewhere that evening. Still, God always strengthened him to get up and take his place in the pulpit. Invariably, the last service was as powerful as the first. He gave it his all. By the time that service ended, I wanted someone to carry me out. But there he was again, heading to the foyer to greet people. In the meantime, I was often hungry, frustrated, and tired of the building. But we kept smiling and greeting.

Eventually we would make it to his office. He would fall on one end of the sofa and I would fall on the other. But God would quickly remind me, "You can't get tired, Everett. You are to give life and hold up his arms. He's exhausted and you've got to serve him." So, I would put on a smile and jump to get some food or whatever I felt he needed. Many times, he would fall asleep within minutes. It was during that time I would check on his family and mine.

Serving the man of God also means serving his family. His wife, the First Lady of the congregation, struggled during services because she could see the pull and effect it had on her husband. It was my job to reassure her that all was well. A good armorbearer knows that if the spouse is happy, the leader will be happy. A good armorbearer needs four eyes (one on God, one on their own family, one on the pastor, and one on the pastor's family.) This mean being constantly on guard and remaining focused.

Sometimes, we wouldn't leave the church until after 6 o'clock in the evening because the pastor fell asleep during the afternoon. I didn't want to wake him because God had ministered in and through him. He needed the rest after twelve or thirteen hour days. Meanwhile, I would just sit and wait (and wait) until he finally woke up. During those waiting periods, I made sure my own family had made it home safely, as well as the pastor's family. But I loved it because it was my calling. To this day, I recall with joy the excitement of those early days as an armorbearer.

It was amazing to see how my pastor was able to deal with the challenges and changes that automatically came with his position. Was everybody pleased with him? No! When God blesses you, it automatically stirs up "haters." I define them as people who don't want to see you blessed. They are the people who say that they are happy for you, but deep inside they are envious and jealous and want you to fail. Success attracts the enemy.

The Pressures of Success

As I saw God take a young man (who had no idea of what it took to pastor a large congregation) from one level to the next, I watched him become overwhelmed with the pressures of that calling. So, how did I deal with serving such a man? I allowed him to be him. The human! Not the one who had to be strong and courageous all day every day. I allowed him to be vulnerable. I realized that he had nowhere to go and just relax. Everyone needs an outlet every now and then. Even the greatest of leaders need to relax. So I attempted to create an atmosphere for him to laugh, joke around, and enjoy life. I wanted to create a balance for him and create times that he could study God's Word without distraction, as well as time with family, and time to enjoy friends and hobbies.

As his acclaim increased, so did the stress and pressure. During that time I said to myself, "Don't ever wish that you were someone else." People would look at my pastor and see how blessed he was with material things and how God had His hands on him. They would say things like, "He is a blessed man," "He has it all together," or "He has no worries." What they didn't see was, were his struggles, bouts with depression and discouragement, and times he wanted to call it quits.

My role included encouraging him that he could do it. When the pressures grew to overwhelming proportions, I reminded him this was God's doing—it wasn't about him. Many people see the glamour of a position, but they were not there when the calling first intensified. There were times that I would tell him that he was like Dr. Jekyll and Mr. Hyde. At one point, it became difficult to keep him focused because he was being pulled in many directions. After all, he was a husband, a father, a pastor, and a leader that others looked to for advice, comfort, direction, and counseling.

Because of the new levels that God was taking him to, it became challenging to serve him. Talk about mood swings. One minute he was happy, the next minute he was sad, the next minute he was crying, and the next minute he laughed like a child. I had to let him be himself and learn not to criticize but encourage. I often reassured him that I understood, although I didn't quite understand all of what was happening in and through him.

Moving from Success to Significance

When God called me to leave that ministry, which I had served for more than a decade, I struggled. It was all I knew. I didn't know how to serve anyone else. I had just reached the point where I could finish his sentences—something I had asked God for in prayer. I wanted to be connected closely to him because he

was on fire for God. I wanted him to prosper and
succeed. I was sold out to the call. "So why leave?"
you may ask. Because I prayed and fasted and heard
God say that it was time for me to go. I cried and
grew quite depressed because I didn't know where
I was going. It wasn't because I had another job. I
didn't have anywhere to go.

Starting in April of 2001, I took a three- month
sabbatical. During that time away I reflected on some
things and received clear direction about what God
wanted me to do. When the time came to end that
sabbatical, I knew that I was not going back. I struggled with fear. When God calls you to step out and
do what He says, it can be quite scary because you
can't see the entire picture. Not only was I scared, I
lost a lot of sleep and weight, which I couldn't afford
to lose. On the day of my scheduled return to the
ministry, a good friend called, telling me I was on his
mind. I told him about the situation. After we talked
for a while, I made up my mind to obey God and
not give in to fear. Although I knew that I had to
obey God anyway, I was allowing my fear to keep
me from obeying. Needless to say, I resigned from
the ministry.

I once heard a statement that there will come
a time when God will move you from success to
significance. During my tenure at my former church,
I trained others to serve the pastor. Since I had taught
them all that I knew and had learned over the years,
the time had come for me to move on. What I didn't
know was that I was going to serve other pastors
and help train others to become armorbearers and

servants. It is my calling. If you are called to serve your pastor, you should study him or her. Get to know the person. Pray for him or her and ask God for wisdom and guidance. Serving is not based on a feeling, but on purpose and calling. It's who you are. If your pastor is overwhelmed, ask God to help you serve His man or woman of God so that you can help them during a trying time.

Study Questions

1. Discuss ways on how you can continue to serve with joy during those times when your leader is not wearing his "Superman" suit.

_____

_____

_____

_____

_____

_____

2. When your leader is unsure or uneasy about a situation, what steps do you take to bring about peace and security?

_____

_____

_____

_____

_____

_____

3. Discuss how you handle situations when those who are close to your pastor begin to drain or annoy him.

_____

_____

_____

_____

_____

_____

4. Discuss the title of this book and its meaning.

_____

_____

_____

_____

_____

_____

5. Discuss the purpose of foot washing.

_____

_____

_____

_____

_____

_____

Chapter 6

Getting Prepared for Blessings

Ever feel as if you are barely hanging on, feeling so desperate it's as if your doctor had come to you and said, "I'm sorry, but we've done all we know how to do." You have made every attempt to hold on to hope. You have repented, tried to forgive, prayed, and cried out to God, yet it feels like no one hears. Since no one sees you, you feel invisible, as if someone hooked you up to life support and left you to die. People have counted you out, leaving you to wonder, "Does anyone care?"

In the midst of this, you can hear what God is saying and know his Word is true, but you have grown cold, numb, and unresponsive. You feel you have no fight left. If you have reached such a state, don't quit! Because of the feelings of despondency and bleakness I have endured—and overcome—I believe that you still have one good punch left in you. It is the blow that will take the devil out and help you break through to freedom. Such a resounding victory will give you the next breath you need to arise.

I recall when I had reached a point of hopelessness. Noticing my countenance and upbeat personality were fading, a pastor from another ministry and some of his advisors had come to talk to me. I shared with them some of the struggles I had experienced. Afterwards, they felt it necessary to tell others some of the things I had divulged in the strictest of confidence. When I realized what they had done, I wanted to expose them as well. Before acting on this impulse, though, I realized I had a choice. I could hold on to hurt and disappointment, or forgive and move on. Thankfully, I chose the latter.

Later, I realized how an ugly scene over this betrayal would have primarily hurt me. From this encounter emerged the lesson that how you exit a ministry is as important as how you enter it. This changed the way that I looked at myself and the way I acted. If I weren't careful, from that point on I could have judged everyone based on the various hurts and damage I had suffered in ministry. I would evaluate every person based on life's slings and arrows. Doing so would have aborted the blessings and miracles God had promised me. Likewise, if you aren't careful, you may find yourself saying and doing things that you may regret later.

Getting Into Position

There are six primary points to getting into position to receive the blessings that God has for you:

1) **Don't hold grudges: "Above all else, guard your heart, for it is the wellspring of life." (Prov. 4:23.)**
   If you have been wounded in a ministry or relationship, you face the danger of a hardened heart, which will poison you with unforgiveness, bitterness, resentment, and anger. Before you depart, make sure you have examined your heart. Forgiveness does not necessarily mean that you ignore the offense, but it does require you to take a penetrating look at yourself to see how you may have contributed to the situation. You can either take responsibility for your actions or hold on to the offense and play the victim.

Forgiveness has nothing to do with the offender and everything to do with you and God.

Besides the betrayal I mentioned earlier, on another occasion a ministry leader deeply hurt me. Though I didn't want to hold on to a grudge, I realized that I needed help letting go of it. I ached to retaliate. I wanted that person to pay for what he had done. To resolve this struggle, I decided to call a friend overseas who is also a pastor. After I described what had happened, he replied, "Until you are able to pray for the person that offended you, you won't be able to be delivered and move on with your life and your purpose."

When he told me that, I had to admit that I couldn't do it. It took years to find the grace to pray for that person and his ministry. During those years of unforgiveness, I developed a victim mentality and became stagnant in my ministry and calling. I was foolish, because each day I kept hearing my friend saying, "You have to forgive so that you can move on with your life." As long as I held on to hurt, bitterness, and anger, I could never go any higher with God or fulfill my calling from Him. Thankfully, I found deliverance and healing. While I gave up that grudge, I have to constantly pray and seek God to stay focused on Him. Human interaction means constant sources of misunderstanding, friction, and conflict.

Dealing with the minefield of human mistakes and emotions means constantly facing the need to apologize and forgive. Using these tools requires that you listen to what God has called you to do. Never mind what you have experienced. While you don't ignore the hurt or offense, you must choose to forgive and let go of grudges. As Ephesians 4:32 advises, "Be kind and compassionate to one another, forgiving each other, just as in Christ God forgave you." Remembering how much God forgave you, don't wait until the offender comes to you to ask for forgiveness (you may be waiting until Christ's return.) Take the high road and forgive first.

2) **Practice patience: "Perseverance must finish its work so that you may be mature and complete, not lacking anything." (James 1:4.)**

A fruit of love, patience is a sign of maturity and trust in God. Patience proves that you care about another person's welfare more than you care about your own. Remember, when you are called to be a servant, that includes caring about another person's dreams and desires first. As you serve another man or woman faithfully, you are trusting God to bring your dreams and vision to pass.

Exercising patience during times of disappointment, hurt, and adversity is a sign of maturity. Every person has been hurt, but the question is whether you will hold on to the disappointment or will you trust God by practicing patience. During the time of my "issues," I found it hard to practice patience and love. I wanted revenge so I could let the offender feel some of the same pain. God never allowed that to happen; I'm thankful that He didn't.

3) **Never get entangled into arguments and disputes: "Do not answer a fool according to his folly, or you will be like him yourself." (Prov. 26:4.)**

When people feel hurt or disappointed, they tend to spew venom, which causes further arguments and disputes. This goes against the wisdom found in Proverbs 29:11, "A fool gives full vent to his anger, but a wise man keeps himself under control." Face it: When you are unhappy with yourself, there is always the tendency to argue with the person that you feel is holding you back or hindering you from accomplishing your dreams. In reality, no one can stop you from achieving your goals but you.

If you're like me, there are times when you allow other people to dictate your happiness. In the past, if someone didn't give me his or her "stamp of approval," I hesitated to move forward. I would argue with both the other person and myself, since I was unhappy with me. You should never allow others to control you this way, including feeling that you have to answer accusations against you that others make up. Even attempting to respond means stirring up additional emotions, draining you of energy and causing you to lose focus of your assignment. You are a gift. The more you see yourself through the eyes of God, the more you will begin to like you for who you are. Eventually, you won't have the time for silly arguments or disputes.

4) **Never give up: "You need to persevere so that when you have done the will of God, you will receive what he has promised." (Heb. 10:36.)**

There are consequences to any decision. Convictions are what will sustain you as you deal with the consequences. This is why it is so important to treat others with the kind of respect that you would like to receive. There will be many opportunities to give up and quit. Before making major, life-altering decisions, consult with God or someone you know will give you godly advice. If you are called to a position, He will either see you through it or direct you to your next assignment. Leaving does not equate with quitting; it can be a sign of strength and maturity. However, how you leave determines your next level.

While you are determining to move ahead, don't give up on others, either. Too often people write others off because they don't see change as quickly as they expect. Humans have a tendency to think that they have been patient long enough and should see a difference in a preconceived period of time. If someone hope to change and experience freedom, they need to experience love instead of judgment. Are you guilty of sitting in the judge's seat?

5) **Don't gossip or engage in negative conversations about your leader or the ministry: "A gentle answer turns away wrath, but a harsh word stirs up anger. The tongue of the wise commends knowledge, but the mouth of the fool gushes folly." (Prov. 15:1-2.)**

You have a responsibility to see to your leader's safety. No armorbearer has a right to meet with a group of people to talk about "how bad things are." If you feel things are that bad, it would be best to leave. Many times people would come to me in an attempt to gain inside information about my pastor. My responsibility was to direct them to him or refer them to Scripture. Strive to avoid speaking to anyone and everyone about your feelings concerning the church. If you must speak with someone, refrain from saying anything unkind or critical.

Over the years I have learned that what I said was less important than how I said it. Words have awesome power. They can start strife or stop it, heal or hurt. I have learned that most people won't come to you with gossip if you always respond by taking them straight to the object of their gossip. Despite this, I have met numerous people who allowed others to influence them to leave a ministry, often based on third-hand information that only bore a small semblance to the truth. If you make a decision to leave a ministry, let it be based on what God reveals to you. Many people have stopped going to church or even searching for a church home because someone fed them negative information about the pastor or the ministry.

6) **Respond in love: "'Love the Lord your God with all your heart and with all your soul and with all your mind.' This is the first and greatest commandment. And the second is like**

it: **'Love your neighbor as yourself."** **(Matt. 22:37-39.)**

In order to guard your heart from judgment, you must accept other people for who they are, simply because they are who God created them to be. If He loves them, so should you. We must love and value others in the same way that God loves us despite our actions, faults, and mistakes. Accepting another person does not necessarily mean that we agree with their behavior. It simply keeps us from sitting in the seat of a judge. The only way that I was able to love, accept, and forgive others was to separate that person's worth from his or her mistakes.

This isn't always easy. I have worked with people who—because of their fear and insecurity—became abusive in their words and actions. There is a normal tendency to want to respond in kind, but what I have discovered is such people are often wounded and hiding behind a gruff exterior. They are frightened by the possibility that the person or persons they are trying to impress may be the very one who may reject them. So, how should you respond to a person who is afraid? You love them to freedom, until they find their worth in God. Don't throw in the towel or lose faith in them. As we show love in a tangible way, the more we will see change in our churches, communities, marriages, and homes.

As we sometimes struggle to accept others, we may face the battle of accepting ourselves. I too have been guilty of feeling bound, trapped, and unworthy, but once I experienced acceptance and worth from God, I no longer felt the need to defend myself.

Because of this, I was able to more quickly respond in love, giving and showing affection. The question is: Are you in love with you?

Can God Count on You?

When John the Baptist baptized Jesus in the Jordan River, the Holy Spirit came down from heaven and rested upon Him as God the Father declared that this was His Son, and He was well pleased with Him. At that time, Jesus had not performed any miracles, nor had He preached or taught the Word. Yet God was well-pleased with Him. Why? Because Jesus had been faithful to love, study, and pray while establishing a close, intimate relationship with His Father. He also honored his earthly parents while developing Godly character. The heavenly Father knew that He could trust Jesus and count on Him in every situation.

What the followers of Christ should strive to achieve is found in Proverbs 16:32, "He who is slow to anger is better than the mighty, and he who rules his spirit, than he who captures a city." (NASB.) I have observed many people who have had opportunities to go far on the journey God has created for them, but because they lacked character and self-control, they lost it all. I once traveled on that road to destruction. I wanted to express how I felt about every situation. If I was not happy about a matter, I verbalized it. It almost cost me my life. If you can't control your temper, you won't be able to control anything that God gives you. He wants to bless you and give you the desires of your heart, but are you ready to handle the blessing? Conquering my run-on tendencies meant putting my flesh in check. No one wants to die to their flesh. But until you are able to deny its cravings, you can forget about pulling down strongholds so you can accomplish and receive all that God has for you. In Joshua 1:8, God says that He wants His children to be "prosperous and successful."

There are many people who have great potential and are looking for that door of opportunity to open. Yet they lack discipline, won't serve, and refuse to fast for even one day so they can hear more clearly from God. David is a great example of how we should prepare for future opportunities. Until he had learned to responsibly and consistently look after his herd of sheep, God could not anoint Him to be king. So, who is standing in your way and blocking your blessing? Is it you? Why can't you advance any further in life? Are you your own worst enemy? Surely it's not God. In John 10:10, Jesus said that He came that we would have abundant life.

When situations arise in your life, can God trust you? When that boss, pastor, spouse, child, or friend hurts you, can He still trust you to do the right thing? Will you still forgive? Will you still serve? Will you still help others to accomplish their dreams? Setbacks, disputes, and adversity all represent a test. Are you going to pass it? There is a constant war between your flesh and your spirit. Will you walk hand in hand with God and resist temptation or go your own selfish way? Temptation is inevitable; I was tempted many times to leave my post and stop serving, to throw in the towel and leave ministry. I didn't need any more headaches. I faced a choice. So do you.

Are You Ready for Your Promotion?

How do you get promoted? Remember, lasting promotion doesn't come from another human being, but from the Lord. This principle is illustrated in the story of Saul's fall from grace, which cost him leadership over Israel: "The Lord said to Samuel, 'How long will you mourn for Saul, since I have rejected him as king over Israel? Fill your horn with oil and be on your way; I am sending you to Jesse of Bethlehem. I have chosen one of his sons to be king.'" (1 Sam. 16:1.)

Because of Saul's rebellion, God rejected him from reigning as king of Israel. God told Samuel that He was taking away the kingdom from Saul and giving it to another man. Before He replaced Saul, though, God had to prepare someone else to rule in his place. What task is God preparing you for? Are you ready for your promotion? People often jockey for position but leave God out of the equation. God chooses the successor. He chooses your position. And He is looking for obedient servants. He wants those who are willing to die to self and say, "Lord, here I am, use me as you want to use me."

Further down in 1 Samuel come these words: "So he asked Jesse, 'Are these all the sons you have?' 'There is still the youngest,' Jesse answered, 'but he is tending the sheep.' Samuel said, 'Send for him; we will not sit down until he arrives.' So he sent and had him brought in. He was ruddy, with a fine appearance and handsome features. Then the Lord said, 'Rise and anoint him; he is the one.' So Samuel took the horn of oil and anointed him in the presence of his brothers, and from that day on the Spirit of the LORD came upon David in power. Samuel then went to Ramah." (v. 11-13.)

Did you catch the significance of this passage? David was out back, faithfully doing what he was called to do. On the verge of greatness he was simply tending sheep and playing his guitar while not complaining about his lowly status. Like I did, this is where many people mess up. Dissatisfied with my armorbearer's position and how things were going, I murmured and complained. God had to deal with me severely. People so often judge by appearances, gifts, talents, and abilities, but God is looking for servants. He wants faithful people who won't complain, even when the going gets tough.

Another way you can receive your promotion is through obedience. David's obedience resulted in him becoming Israel's champion. Too many people miss out on blessings and promotions because they want to pray and never act, when God has told His children to do something. There are some things that you don't have to pray about; you just have to obey God. David was faithful, no matter how boring, mundane, or insignificant the task seemed. As long as you obey God, He is more than faithful, even in life-threatening situations. This can be seen in the following story David told Saul about his past:

"But David said to Saul, 'Your servant has been keeping his father's sheep. When a lion or a bear came and carried off a sheep from the flock, I went after it, struck it and rescued the sheep from its mouth. When it turned on me, I seized it by its hair, struck it and killed it. Your servant has killed both the lion and the bear; this uncircumcised Philistine will be like one of them, because he has defied the armies of the living God. The Lord who delivered me from the paw of the lion and the paw of the bear will deliver me from the hand of this Philistine.' Saul said to David, 'Go, and the Lord be with you.'" (1 Samuel 17:34-37.)

Again I ask: Are you in position to receive your promotion, breakthrough, healing, deliverance, or financial miracle? One way you can get there is by entering a place of submission and taking orders from those who are in authority over you. First Samuel 17:20-22 illustrates how David while he was still in the position of a shepherd: "Early in the morning David left the flock with a shepherd, loaded up and set out, as Jesse had directed. He reached the camp as the army was going out to its battle positions, shouting the war cry. Israel and the Philistines were drawing up their lines facing each other. David left his things with the keeper of supplies, ran to the battle lines and greeted his brothers."

David was a "detail" person who noticed everything. Although excited and enthusiastic, he didn't allow it to distract him from being obedient and responsible for his assignment. He passed his tests. What tests have you passed? When you receive an assignment, do you perform it with excitement and enthusiasm? Do you pay attention to the little details? Or are you walking around harboring a negative attitude toward your leader?

Many times I was asked to perform tasks that didn't necessarily make me happy, but I knew that God had given me an assignment. In order to be blessed, I had to submit to authority. I recall the late night hours of prayer, as well as the times I rubbed sleep from my eyes to intercede for my pastor. I remember the days of fasting and seeking the Lord, asking Him to protect and cover my leader. I did so because I wanted my promotion. I wanted the hand of God to remain on my life. The questions you must ponder are: How bad do you want to be promoted? How desperate are you to keep the hand of God on your life?

Study Questions

1. Why is it important that you guard your heart from unforgiveness?

_____

_____

_____

_____

_____

_____

2. How long should you give a person to change?

_____

_____

_____

_____
_____

3. What steps are you willing to take to show someone that you love them?

_____
_____
_____
_____
_____
_____

4. Share with others a test that you have passed. Describe how that makes you feel.

_____
_____
_____
_____
_____
_____

5. What steps are you taking to get into position for your promotion?

_____
_____
_____
_____
_____

Chapter 7

Unity Commands Blessings

"How good and pleasant it is when brothers live together in unity! It is like precious oil poured on the head, running down on the beard, running down on Aaron's beard, down upon the collar of his robes. It is as if the dew of Hermon were falling on Mount Zion. For there the Lord bestows his blessing, even life forevermore."
Psalm 133:1-3

As long as the devil can keep the Church separated and divided, he knows that he can defeat us. He is constantly striving to build walls in our relationships by persuading us to get upset over irrelevant, minute, and insignificant details. During my years of service as an armorbearer, many people have attempted to spoil the relationships between my overseers and me. While many failed, some succeeded. Whenever there is insecurity in a church, attempts will often come to divide people. That is the devil's plan.

Yet, over the years I have also learned that that there is nothing that can stop a ministry, a marriage, a community, a church, or an organization that is unified. When there is unity, victory will come. As long as there is discord and dissention within a church, a home, a ministry or an organization, God will not bless you. You can shout, run, jump, and holler until midnight. God will not listen as long as there is disunity. Many have been deceived by the enemy. Satan can find entry points through your personality, vocabulary, religion, gender, or race. He uses all of what you are familiar with to separate you from those around you. He fears you achieving unity with them.

Nor does he stop with your personal traits. The devil pretends to be the Holy Spirit in a language that you understand. If you are African-American, he tells you to not to talk to Caucasians because "you can't trust them." If you're a Republican, he tells you not to listen to Democrats. If you're a Pentecostal, he tells you to avoid Baptists, Methodists, and those of other denominations. He uses whatever he can to cause division. The troubling thing is that many people fail to recognize this tactic and fall prey to his schemes.

Unity Intimidates the Enemy

The enemy gets intimidated when he sees a church, a family, a community, a company, or an organization working in covenant unity. That puts him on the run. To counter-attack, he will constantly remind people of their past, hurt, disappointments, pain, or other things that held them in bondage. He does this because he knows that once people are free and walking in agreement with their brothers and sisters, they will be unstoppable.

There are some areas of life where you are not called to function alone. You need strong brothers and sisters who are in covenant with you and will stand by you so you can accomplish your assignment. Psalm 84:6-7 describes such a unity: "As they pass through the Valley of Baca, they make it a place of springs; the autumn rains also cover it with pools. They go from strength to strength, till each appears before God in Zion."

Notice from this passages that the ones who go through difficult and challenging times, which helps them develop strength and discover life, will reach their destination. If you have successfully weathered some storms in your life, recognize that you owe a great measure of your success to faithful people who helped you. This unity made the difference. In my life I have had success and made a lot of progress. As I look back, I realize that much of the credit goes to the men and women God placed in my life to help me. My advice to anyone who desires to accomplish anything of significance is to never attempt it alone. You need other men and women who are going to pray, cover you, and watch out for your safety.

If we are going to accomplish anything in life, we have to have strong people around us who will hold us accountable and tell us the truth. Sometimes we can get religious. Instead of being faithful to the task, we put on a show to make others think we're following God when in truth we're fulfilling our own desires. Such actions disqualify us. God is looking for faithful people who will stay the course.

Who Are You?

Before there can be unity in a church or other organization, each person must know his or her identity. So I ask: Who are you? When I was growing up, and even earlier in my adult life, people often compared my performances to others. If mine didn't measure up to their standards, they criticized or mocked me. Needless to say, I developed an inferiority complex and the mindset that I wasn't "good enough." When I attempted to do my best, but others criticized me, put me down, or rejected me, I felt like an utter failure.

With this kind of outlook, I struggled to feel like part of a team. I would often isolate myself so that I couldn't make any more noticeable mistakes. No matter how hard I tried, I still felt that someone would not be satisfied. I would think, "If I could do something great, I would be accepted by God and others." Wrong! This concept left me feeling burned out, lonely, depressed, and more confused. It was not until I accepted myself and recognized that God loved me no matter what others thought. I no longer lived my life to please other people. Yes, I wanted them to like me, but if they didn't, that was their loss.

What I came to realize was that until I found out who I was, I could not be a blessing to anyone else, let alone an effective armorbearer. In the past, to fill that void in my life, I would often try to over-compensate for my personal identity with what I did. Many people spend a good part of their lives trying to live up to others' expectations while constantly feeling bad about themselves. The source of such self-loathing is the devil. He wants all people to be more concerned with *what we do* than *who we are*. As groups of people, how do we become a unified unit? By knowing who we are.

Many people walk around looking for affirmation and encouragement from their parents, pastors, bosses, spouses, children, and friends. When they don't receive that affirmation, or receive what they see as inadequate amounts, they feel deeply flawed and wounded. They think they have some kind of psychological or social issue, but what they really need, is love, acceptance, and forgiveness.

When I resigned from the ministry that I served for many years to go elsewhere, they loved, accepted, and forgave me. They embraced me and wished me well. The pastor and members affirmed me, assuring me that I was important and had a place in God's Kingdom. Not because of what I could do, but because of who I am.

This is the same kind of love, compassion, and understanding that is available to every child of God. Hebrews 4:15-16 assures us that Jesus knows how we feel and is always there for us: "For we do not have a high priest who is unable to sympathize with our weaknesses, but we have one who has been tempted in every way, just as we are—yet was without sin. Let us then approach the throne of grace with confidence, so that we may receive mercy and find grace to help us in our time of need."

As this passage says, God knows and understands our weaknesses. He is familiar with our fears, doubts, and wrong thinking, and yet He accepts us. The truth is that our acceptance by God rests on Christ's performance, not ours. So, you can rest in the fact that God loves you for who you are.

Have you ever felt pressure to be like someone else? At one time, I was so unhappy with myself that I tried to be like anybody who appeared to be successful. That is, until I heard one man's story. While I was so busy trying to be like him, he was trying to be like someone else. He, too, was unhappy. Talk about confusing! Everybody was trying to be like someone else, making me wonder if anyone was comfortable with themselves. Here I was, constantly running around trying to please other people and be like them, thinking that would fulfill me. Instead, I experienced heartache. One day I took a long look in the mirror and asked, "Everett, who wants to be around someone that is insecure?" Now, I do what I do simply because I love it, not for someone else's approval. I finally fell in love with me.

As Christians we should not compete and compare. We are called to love and not be jealous or envious. We all should be free to love, accept, and forgive others without feeling pressure to compete or compare. Secure, strong people who know who they are in God are not intimidated or threatened by others' gifts and talents. Instead, they compliment others and enjoy what they are doing because they appreciate their own abilities and limitations. As Galatians 5:26 says, "Let us not become boastful, challenging one another, envying one another." (NASB.)

Reaching Your Destiny

Everyone has a calling and a destiny. Your calling and purpose was God's will for you before He spoke the foundations of the earth into existence. Just because you know that God has a plan for your life doesn't mean that it's just going to happen. You have to work at it and cultivate it. You may go through some things while God develops, molds, and builds character in you. You may experience setbacks and disappointments before you ever operate in that calling. Don't throw in the towel and quit before you reach your destiny.

Will Satan attempt to get you to abort the plan of God for your life? Of course. That's his plan. He wants to destroy your confidence. He hopes to steal your inner peace. The minute you decided to follow Jesus, he became angry with you and determined to rattle your cage. He hates you.

I recall a time when I was leading worship and the pastor mentioned to some of the other singers that he wanted another person to take over my position. When I heard that comment, I was distraught. The devil played a scenario of failure over and over in my head until he nearly beat me to a pulp. Whenever I would get up to lead worship, I would freeze up emotionally. The devil had set out to ruin my ministry and me. In the midst of these attacks, I thought, "I'll never be able to lead worship again. I can never stand in front of a group again and sing." If someone got up and left the sanctuary while I was singing, such comments would echo through my mind. It wasn't until I had got alone with God that He affirmed me.

Hebrews 3:6 says to "hold on to our courage and the hope of which we boast." I had to learn to embrace confidence, not because another person said to, but because God told me so. I had to learn to be confident about my gifts, talents, abilities, and calling. I had to constantly encourage myself in God, knowing that He called me, not a human.

Whether you are an armorbearer, choir member, church secretary, or serve in some other capacity, I encourage you to be confident in your calling. Be confident with who you are and bold in God. You are victorious, not a victim. Remember, you have to work on confidence daily and decide to possess it. Don't engage in self-doubt any longer. You have what it takes to succeed and prosper. All you have to do is believe in the power of Him who raised Christ from the dead.

I once heard a statement that helped change my outlook: "A man becomes what he thinks about." Or, as Proverbs 23:7 (KJV) puts it, "For as he thinketh in his heart, so is he." I had to change my thoughts about myself. By taking on what others said about me, I had started believing the negative gossip spread by naysayers. I had to learn to like me and fall in love with myself. Today, I can sing and shout for the Lord and could care less on who says what or who gets up and walks out. It isn't that I have become cocky. I have become confident.

What is God calling you to do in His service that you are afraid to step out and try to do? And all because of what you heard in the past? I once heard someone say, "Don't be afraid of trying and failing, be afraid of succeeding at doing the wrong thing." Many times we allow our fears to torment us, which prevents us from stepping out. You may make a few mistakes, but so what? Get up and keep trying. I have made many mistakes, but I keep trying and pushing.

Remember the parable of the talents that Jesus told in Matthew 25:14-30. The Master in the parable represents God the Father. When the Master distributed talents, the third servant buried his talent because he was afraid. God got very angry with him.

Why? Because he didn't even try. When God asked him about it, he responded that he was afraid. Don't repeat this mistake. God has given you gifts and abilities. There is no reason to fear. Take the chance. As the familiar Nike commercial says, "Just do it!"

In order to become all that God has called you to become, you have to get rid of the weight and the naysayers. Get rid of those things that hinder you and prevent you from running your fastest. Who or what is in your way? Get rid of it. You have a race to win. Follow the advice of Hebrews 12:1: "Therefore, since we are surrounded by such a great cloud of witnesses, let us throw off everything that hinders and the sin that so easily entangles, and let us run with perseverance the race marked out for us."

As I mentioned previously, at one time I ran with people who didn't want me to win. They were what I like to call "blood suckers." Running with the wrong companions can leave you in the dust. Better to follow Paul's instructions to the Corinthians: "Do you not know that in a race all the runners run, but only one gets the prize? Run in such a way as to get the prize. Everyone who competes in the games goes into strict training. They do it to get a crown that will not last; but we do it to get a crown that will last forever. Therefore I do not run like a man running aimlessly; I do not fight like a man beating the air. No, I beat my body and make it my slave so that after I have preached to others, I myself will not be disqualified for the prize." (1 Cor. 9:24-27.)

How bad do you want to win? You can't wait for somebody else to win it for you. You have to run your own race, which takes discipline. Even when you find yourself in difficult and challenging times, you can still experience blessings when your strength is in God. Each of us must keep our hearts and mind on Him and not on circumstances. As I mentioned earlier, when I faced fear or failure I had to control my thoughts. You will encounter similar battles. Satan will constantly whisper, "Things will never change. They won't get better. Your blessings will never come. Your finances will never get better." Don't listen to these lies. Keep your mind set on God.

Success Can Spell Trouble

When you achieve a certain level of success, get ready for trouble. Before ascending to the throne of Israel, David had to endure numerous difficulties. Jealous of his success and fearing the people's hearts were more loyal to David, Saul pursued him and tried to kill him. Ironically, this came after Saul had set him over his soldiers and David had gained acceptance in the sight of Israel. Most people would think this kind of achievement would mean happiness, satisfaction, and contentment. Instead, it brought opposition:

"When the men were returning home after David had killed the Philistine, the women came out from all the towns of Israel to meet King Saul with singing and dancing, with joyful songs and with tambourines and lutes. As they danced, they sang: 'Saul has slain his thousands, and David his tens of thousands.' Saul was very angry; this refrain galled him. 'They have credited David with tens of thousands,' he thought, 'but me with only thousands. What more can he get but the kingdom?' And from that time on Saul kept a jealous eye on David." (1 Sam. 18:6-9.)

There is a modern-day application to this story. What do you do when those close to you want to destroy you? What do you do when you've done nothing wrong, but others threaten your well-being daily? And your boss, spouse, pastor, or children are giving you grief, or no longer trust you? David was faithful to God, a quality that spelled success and victory. Do you want to be successful? Remain faithful. Yes, you will attract haters, but remain faithful. You're on an assignment. Notice that David was not promised anything for being faithful. He was just doing what he knew to do. By obediently tending sheep, his leader placed him in an exalted position.

Obedience and sacrifice may still bring perse-cution. Just because you're successful, that doesn't mean that you are exempt from trouble. It is often just the opposite. I have often heard people say "I'm doing this for God" or, "I'm trying this for God." Don't try anything for God, just be faithful and obedient. I have observed many people looking over their shoulder to see if someone was going to take their position. I used to be the same way. But if God gave it to you, only He can take it away. He doesn't do that unless you're like Saul—rebellious, unfaithful, and unwilling to repent for your actions.

When David achieved success, it tested all of his relationships. Are you ready for your relationships to be tested? Can you still function in your calling if people walk out on you? Success will bring about change in every area of our lives. I once heard the question asked, "Can you stand to be blessed?" Many people are afraid to be blessed because they can't take the criticism that comes with it.

I recall when I purchased the vehicle that I drive now. Initially, I hesitated to drive it, fearful about what others might think or say. I was also hesitant to let others know what community I lived in because I didn't want to hear any negative chatter. Looking back, I wonder why. When you are faithful, God can't help blessing you. I no longer apologize for my blessings. Nor should you. Remember God placed you in these situations.

The Importance of Covenants

While many in America focus excessive attention on money, there are numerous qualities and traits in life that are much more valuable, particularly close, covenant relationships like the kind that David and Jonathan enjoyed. This passage from 1 Samuel spells it out:

"'Come,' Jonathan said, 'let's go out into the field.' So they went there together. Then Jonathan said to David: 'By the Lord, the God of Israel, I will surely sound out my father by this time the day after tomorrow! If he is favorably disposed toward you, will I not send you word and let you know? But if my father is inclined to harm you, may the Lord deal with me, be it ever so severely, if I do not let you know and send you away safely. May the Lord be with you as he has been with my father. But show me unfailing kindness like that of the Lord as long as I live, so that I may not be killed, and do not ever cut off your kindness from my family—not even when the Lord has cut off every one of David's enemies from the face of the earth.' So Jonathan made a covenant with the house of David, saying, 'May the Lord call David's enemies to account.' And Jonathan had David reaffirm his oath out of love for him, because he loved him as he loved himself." (1 Sam. 20:1-17.)

The unity forged by such covenants is the only thing that will stand in times of testing. When you are facing storms, difficulties, and challenges, you need covenant relationships. As you mature in God and achieve success, your relational standards must change. You need to build covenants. Jonathan knew that God had anointed David for leadership. He wasn't crazy. Jonathan wanted to make covenant with an anointed vessel. Don't get hooked up with somebody who lacks God's anointing. If you have to question whether a person is following Christ, leave him or her alone.

However, don't expect everything to run smoothly—or everyone to be happy—because you form covenants. Don't be surprised if someone (possibly in authority) reacts as Saul did: "Saul's anger flared up at Jonathan and he said to him, 'You son of a perverse and rebellious woman! Don't I know that you have sided with the son of Jesse to your own shame and to the shame of the mother who bore you? As long as the son of Jesse lives on this earth, neither you nor your kingdom will be established. Now send and bring him to me, for he must die!'" (1 Sam. 20:30-31.) Seeing his father's anger, Jonathan knew that by supporting David he would likely never become king. He loved David at his own expense. He was willing to love at the cost of losing everything he had, knowing he wouldn't gain a thing.

Are you willing to give up everything you have in order to make a covenant with someone you know God has anointed? I'm not talking about convenience. Convenient love is when you are in it for yourself. Covenant love is when you don't care about anything except what God cares about. You have nothing to gain.

I have seen people gather together solely for business purposes, or take political positions to gain favor or promote their ministry. God is nowhere in such equations. Watch who comes into your presence. Take note of who always wants to be around you; check their motives. I have seen people cast out devils, prophesy, declare blessings, and perform healings and deliverance. But it wasn't always for

God's glory. God is looking for those who will lay down their lives for others, just as Jesus did. Are you that person? Can God count on you? Are you willing to die to yourself and lay down your life for another soul? This is the kind of armorbearers the Church needs.

Study Questions

1. What steps are you taking to become secure with who you are?

_____

_____

_____

_____

_____

_____

2. How would you describe the relationship between David and Jonathan? What would such a relationship mean to you?

_____

_____

_____

_____

_____

_____

3. Why was Saul displeased with David? Is anyone jealous of your achievements? Why?

_____

_____

_____

_____

_____

_____

4. If you were David, discuss with the group how you would have handled the situation with Jonathan and Saul?

_____

_____

_____

_____

_____

5. Who is your covenant partner? What difference has this relationship made?

_____

_____

_____

_____

_____

6. Discuss with the group a particular area where you are afraid to step out and do what God called you to do.

_____

_____

_____

_____

_____

Chapter 8

How to Keep Your Armorbearer

While it happened before my time, I remember my pastor telling me about Floyd Patterson coming back from a humiliating defeat to whip Ingemar Johansson for the heavyweight championship in 1960. Decked multiple times in their first match, the next time out Patterson fought smarter, wearing out Johansson's mid-section until he had weakened him enough to land a stunning blow to his chin. With his body weakened, the big Swede was ripe for defeat.

In their rematch, Patterson kept his guard up to protect his face from getting hit while wearing out his opponent's body, deflecting Johansson's counter punching with tremendous pressure. In the fifth round, Patterson knocked the fighter down for the first time in his career before polishing him off with a ferocious left hook that left him lying on the canvas.

The church can be compared to a boxing match. If the body (the church) isn't strong enough, the head (the pastor) will constantly try to protect the body from attack by the opponent (the devil.) However, if the body remains strong through such techniques as reading the Word, studying, praying and fasting, the head can focus on the opponent's moves and plan counterattacks. The body can stand longer, make his moves, dodge when necessary, and gain the victory as long as the head is focused.

Today, the church is in a weakened state. Examining the developing trend of empty pulpits, I can't help wondering what calamities await the next generation. While churches close down, casinos, drugs, and the pornography industry flourish. Unless we produce quality church planters and raise up godly leaders who can effectively lead God's Kingdom, we will inevitably find ourselves with childish leaders who have few clues about their purpose.

There is a desperate cry for new faces and voices to come forward so the church can remain effective. I often say if you see the enemy coming, you can plan for the attack by creating strategies for victory. However, the subtle attack on the church is like a flame slowly dwindling while few notice the fire sputtering out. There is no longer joy or passion in the relationship because people are caught up in life's day-to-day routine. One day they may realize they have the lost the One who was there to help them and, as a result, are dead inside.

Pastors, just as you need armorbearers, they need you. They need to know you care and that they add value to your life. Too many armorbearers are experiencing burnout while pastors act as if everything is okay. Take time out for them, which is how you will keep them motivated and committed. People don't care how much you know until they know how much you care.

Cold & Distant Shepherds

For years others asked me to write a book about serving. Initially, I was reluctant to proceed because of the wounds I felt were inflicted by those I had been called to serve. I didn't want to speak or write out of anger. I first needed healing and deliverance. Not that everything was my pastors' fault, but I had grown bitter, angry, and resentful of the fact that—out of all the sleepless nights and daily sacrifices I made to be a true armorbearer and good servant—my shepherds could be so cold, distant, and unappreciative.

Still, God kept reminding me that He had called me, not a man. He called me to serve Him through man. Sadly, though, many armorbearers are not stepping up and doing what they have been called to do because pastors are not doing their job. After all, who wants to give 100 percent when you feel you're only getting 25 percent back? Who wants to give their all when they feel abused or unappreciated?

As I see it, a leading problem today is that pastors are not covering their armorbearers in prayer. Since they don't have their best interests at heart, it is hard to find a true armorbearer. Armorbearers regularly tell me that they feel as if they don't matter, as if they are figurative doormats. Pastors, what are you doing? Do you care about those who are serving you? Are you so caught up into yourself that you can't appreciate those who are looking out for you?

Remember how Saul felt about David. Despite the animosity that eventually overtook him, at first Saul loved David dearly. One of the challenges today is that some pastors don't love their armorbearers. Instead, they are using and manipulating them. How do we stop this vicious cycle? By taking care of the gifts that God has given us. We start by dying to self and seeking God's will for our lives. We start by acknowledging the fact that everybody can't lead. Somebody must follow, serve, and take orders.

Let me add a word of caution: We should never so moody to the point that one day you want your servant close to you and the next day you are skeptical of him or her. And the day after that, you aren't speaking to him and the next day, you act cold. Be consistent. You can't have it both ways. You can't act one way on one day, another way the next, and expect your armorbearer to know what box you're coming out of today. As Colossians 3:21 says, "Fathers, do not embitter your children, or they will become discouraged."

If a problem has occurred, or if your armorbearer has made some kind of mistake, communicate that to your servant. That way, no one will have to walk around on eggshells. It is hard to serve when you're not sure what to say or do. If you want a committed armorbearer, he or she must be close to you and feel comfortable around you.

In addition, don't disrespect your spouse or family in the presence of your armorbearer and expect your armorbearer to respect them later. Your actions will come back to haunt you. You have a responsibility to your servants. The reason so many servants are quitting and leaving their leaders out to dry is because of the latter's selfishness and self-centeredness. I often tell pastors to make sure that you take care of those who are taking care of you.

Concerned About Your Servant's Dreams

Are you concerned about your servant's dreams, hopes, and aspirations? Do you care if they succeed at their calling? Do you have their family's best interest at heart? Leaders sometime lose focus of their assignment to feed the flock because they get caught up in having servants around them. While it is easy to fall prey to hype and attention, you won't have them around for long if they feel mistreated. They will leave you! Not everybody is like David. Somebody will kill you and expose you. People want to go where they are celebrated, not barely tolerated.

There is no greater joy your armorbearers receive than when they are given the opportunity to serve you. But you are called to look after the flock. If your armorbearer feels like he or she is not taken care of or appreciated, eventually your armorbearer will either leave you or only serve you half-heartedly.

Just like their armorbearers, pastors must be reliable, dependable, trustworthy, and know how to maintain a confidence. If you betray your armorbearer, that person's service to you will diminish. No one, especially your armorbearer, wants to be ignored, rejected, or mistreated. As the Bible teaches, do unto others as you would have them do unto you. Communicate to those who serve you.

Although we armorbearers receive joy in serving, in the case of a selfish, self-centered pastor there is no greater relief we receive than when the time comes that we leave that person's presence. Know that your leadership is a privilege given to you by your followers. You have been given a great responsibility. Jesus inspired his chosen followers so much that they left their businesses—and for a time, their families—in order to follow him. He never threatened them or forced them to go. He inspired them.

My question to you is: Are you inspiring those who are following you or are you taking advantage of your position? I know that we as armorbearers must be careful with the close friendships we form, but I suggest that you too be careful. You can't befriend just anyone and expect your armorbearer to remain silent when he or she sees that you are heading in the wrong direction.

Keep in mind that we have been called to submit to your leadership. If we sense that you have closed your ears to us, and no longer want to communicate with us, we will no longer speak about what bothers us. We are to provide strength and bring peace, not introduce strife and contention. This situation alone can cause problems.

Too often pastors will refuse to listen to their servants and begin to operate in their own flesh and fall into something that is detrimental to not only them, but to those around them. When that happens, your armorbearer can no longer protect you. Over the years I have seen pastors grow weary, quit, and even die prematurely because they were doing too much and not focusing on their assignment. Pastors are human and need to be able to enjoy ministering, preaching, and teaching. And, at the same time they should enjoy their lives without the fear of someone trying to bring them down because they are walking in a divine purpose.

Treat Others with Respect

Although your armorbearer is called to serve and protect you, you have a responsibility to God for your words and actions. You should treat others with respect as people who are created in the image and likeness of God. Woe unto you if you take advantage of the one that God sent to serve you, or use your armorbearer to cover up your messes. God sees you and what you're doing. He sees what's happening behind the closed doors. I have heard many pastors say "touch not my anointed…" While that may be true, don't you believe that your amorbearer is anointed to carry out his or her tasks?

Pastors must show the same respect for their servants that they expect their elder boards or church councils to show for them. I can see why pastors must have board members or other accountability systems. While everyone knows their own strengths and weaknesses, they are often reluctant to acknowledge the latter exist. This is why a wise governing board can help the church function. A board that understands its purpose is a board to be praised, for they grasp that their job is not to "run" the pastor or the church. They are to help walk alongside the pastor, support him or her, and help carry the ministry's vision.

This issue of respect goes in all directions. Pastors shouldn't travel around the world regularly and leave the people that God has entrusted them with in someone else's care. Pastors who are always gone should become evangelists and stop trying to lead a local church. They are wounding innocent sheep. I do believe that pastors are gifts and they should travel to teach and help others, but it's almost impossible for a local church body to follow a vision that isn't clearly stated, or is rarely shared from the pulpit. Remember the words of wisdom from Habbakuk 2:2 says, "Then the Lord replied: 'Write down the revelation and make it plain on tablets so that a herald may run with it, write the vision and make it plain.'"

You have to spend some time with those who have been called to serve you. Spend time speaking into your staff. First Ladies, spend some time with staff members' wives, staff women, and the women of the church. Pastors must especially remember to spend time with their armorbearers. They too need attention. They too have challenges and want to talk about their struggles. If they can't come to you, where can they go? Lay hands on your armorbearers, pray over them, and affirm them. If you don't do it, the devil will bring the wrong person into their path.

It would behoove you to do this because if the wrong person gets hooked up with your armorbearer, it will eventually affect you. Most armorbearers that I have met love doing what they are doing. Yet problems arise when they feel mistreated and exploited. What do hurting people do? They hurt people. Remember, you can't give what you don't have. If you don't have joy, you can't give joy. If you don't have peace, you can't give peace. If you don't have compassion, you can't give compassion. If you know that you have hurt or offended your armorbearer, go to him or her and straighten it all out. It will be worth it.

Remember that not everyone who comes into your life who says, "I've been called to be your security officer, your armorbearer, and your intercessor," is called. Yes, they may have good intentions, but how many of you know that the road to hell is paved with good intentions? You must know that you know that they have been called by God to serve you.

It is critical that you treat your armorbearer with the respect and appreciation that this person deserves. I'm not saying that you have to walk around patting them on the back always saying "good job," or "wonderful how you paid attention," and other such remarks. If your armorbearer needs that much attention, he or she needs to check and see if they are in the right position. Still, that isn't a license to disregard their feelings.

In addition, you can't be so insecure that you fail to communicate with those who have been called to serve you. I have seen pastors who didn't know who they were in Christ push away the very one that God sent to help them implement their vision. Yes, they are good "pulpiteers," preachers, teachers, and administrators, but they are insecure with themselves. It is tough to serve and give to you when you are too insecure to receive good treatment and service.

Too often pastors refuse to listen to their servants and begin to operate in their own flesh and motives and fall into something that is detrimental to not only them, but those around them. When that happens, your armorbearer can no longer protect you.

Pastors, you have been given the power to influence through inspiration, not manipulation. You face serious dangers as a leader when you fail to answer to anyone. Your armorbearer wants to protect you. The protection of our pastor is in voluntary submission to a *trusted* authority. One of the reasons servants are growing weary and not covering pastors like they should is because they have been abused, rejected, and mistreated. I pray that this won't be your legacy.

Serving is a Two-Way Street

Stop and think for a moment: What if you were serving you? How would you feel? Would you appreciate you? As I serve my present leader, I often remind myself to serve others like I would want others to serve me. No one likes to feel mistreated or unappreciated. Therefore, I must not mistreat others. Now that you have thought about that for a moment, how do you feel? Would you still be in the ministry?

Those who are leading must also serve. As I mentioned earlier, he who is greatest among you is your servant. As you go through life's journey, skills and wills must be developed. If a leader ever loses heart and forget that service is an honor and privilege, they cease to build God's Kingdom and start to build their own. Yes, I believe in giving honor to whom honor is due, but I also believe that the ones who are being served should never get too comfortable being served. Never forget where you were when God picked you up. Many leaders forget their moment of desperation. Therefore, they lose sight of taking the hands of those who are now serving them, pulling them up and affirming them.

Part of the reason God takes us through wilderness experiences is to teach us so that we will not get distracted from the lessons life brings. Never forget your small beginnings, the people who invested in you in those early years, or the encouragers and motivators who believed in you when you didn't believe in yourself. Never forget those who mentored you when you didn't see the gifts that God had placed in you, but they pushed and encouraged you to keep moving forward. Your armorbearer needs that same mentorship from you. Now it's your time to be that person, pushing someone else to move forward.

I have spoken with many armorbearers who, like I was, felt left alone to rot. My suggestion to leaders is to never let the pressing crowd trick you into thinking that they are the ones who made you important enough to be celebrated. It was that servant who prayed you through when you wanted to quit and those individuals who encouraged you and told you that you could make it. How do you keep your armorbearer? By letting them know that you are grateful for their sacrifices. Your journey, our journey, is where God trains us and builds our character.

I once heard someone say, "The crowd loves what you give to them, but an armorbearer loves you even in your struggles." Even in our struggles, we must remember the ones who were there with us. Don't get me wrong: I'm not saying that you should always look back to pull those along with you. But I do believe that armorbearers don't mind staying in the ring to fight battles, as long as they know that their leader is not going to leave them during battle. Have you ever seen a child in athletics or other competitions? They perform better when their parents are there supporting them. Your armorbearer doesn't mind serving as long as they have the support of their leader.

Pastors who aren't careful can easily turn their armorbearers into entourages. Armorbearers are given to you by God as warriors. They are placed at your side to help fight the real battles, not groupies who sashay with you through the crowds to make you look prominent. Remember what Proverbs 16:18 days, "Pride goes before destruction, a haughty spirit before a fall." Everyone is subject to temptations. Even the mighty men in the Old and New Testaments had a thorn in their flesh that buffeted them. None of us are above the struggles or temptations of weakness. We must never get arrogant in our anointing.

Remember when Jesus washed His disciples' feet? He could have done or said so many things that would have left a lasting impression on them, but He chose to wash their feet. Think about what were in the minds of those twelve men as Jesus girded himself with a towel and kneeled down to wash their feet with a servant's heart. If we truly believe that leadership begins at the top, then leaders who are being served must ask themselves if they are humbled enough to wash the feet of those who are helping lift their load.

Leaders who have a servant's heart will most likely surround themselves with other servants or armorbearers. Leaders who are more into the glamour or being served than serving others will have entourages. Which one do you want to be known as keeping? Which leaves the question: how do you keep your armorbearer? Serve them while they serve you.

Study Questions

1. How can you as a pastor assure your armorbearer that you truly care about their dreams, family and goals?

_____

_____

_____

_____

_____

_____

2. Can your armorbearer be honest with you without fear of being exposed or mistreated? Why or why not?

_____

_____

_____

_____

_____

_____

3. Do you encourage, motivate or inspire those who serve you? How?

_____

_____

_____

_____

_____

_____

4. Have you taken your armorbearer for granted? If not, what advice can you give to other leaders?

_____

_____

_____

_____

_____

5. Armorbearers, if you don't feel respected by your pastor, how can you seek to correct that situation?

_____

_____

_____

_____

_____

Printed in the United States
120915LV00001B/128/P